quick and easy
container gardening

quick and easy
container gardening

20 step-by-step projects and inspirational ideas

TESSA EVELEGH

photography by DEBBIE PATTERSON

CICO BOOKS

LONDON NEW YORK

Published in 2008 by CICO Books
an imprint of Ryland Peters & Small
20–21 Jockey's Fields, London WC1R 4BW

www.cicobooks.co.uk

10 9 8 7 6 5 4 3 2 1

A CIP catalogue record for this book is available from the British Library.

ISBN-13: 978 1 906094 39 3
ISBN-10: 1 906094 39 X

Printed in China

Editor: Gillian Haslam
Designer: Christine Wood
Photographer: Debbie Patterson

CONTENTS

INTRODUCTION

Containers overflowing with glorious hues bring joy to the garden, concentrating colour and interest just where you want it. They are a glorious moveable feast. A favourite shrub just finished flowering? Then brighten up what might have become a dull spot with a container full of the season's best blooms. Having an outdoor celebration? Then bring on the containers for instant patio decoration.

But the real appeal of containers is that they offer instant gardening. Pot them up in less than an hour, and immediately you have concentrated colour with the promise that this is only going to get better over the next few weeks, months and even years, depending on the plants. That's manageable for even the busiest of us, and it's do-able, even if our only outside space is a balcony.

And when one growing season has finished, you can easily move tired containers to a quiet spot in the garden for rest and recuperation, while instantly filling the vacated space with a new display using the new season's latest look. On a more permanent design note, containers can bring focus both to the house and garden. For example,

BELOW: The joyous primary yellows of Iceland poppies can be concentrated together in containers to provide lively impressionist colour in the garden.

BELOW RIGHT: Summer's favourite bedding plants, such as petunias and verbenas, come in a wide range of colours, providing plenty of scope for planting a container that complements the planting in the rest of the garden.

you can smarten an entrance with a pair of elegant matching containers, planted with evergreen trees or topiary.

In this book, you'll find a wealth of information on planting up different kinds of containers and cossetting them into a glorious show. If you want something fun and frivolous, then turn to the 'Party Pots' chapter, where you'll find plenty of decorative entertaining ideas; if you're an eco-warrior, glean some ideas from the 'Junk Genius' chapter on recycled containers, or concentrate on 'Drought Busters' containers. Hot on sustainability? Try growing your own 'Crops in Pots'.

As well as seasonal annual plantings, there's a wealth of ideas designed to be more enduring, and even suggestions as to how to refresh their looks over the years. Backed up by all the practical planting and care details you'll need for success, most importantly this book is about the sheer enjoyment of container gardening. It looks at planting in an imaginative way that considers the overall creation: pots, plants and positioning working together to create impact in the garden. Enjoy!

BELOW: Pretty modest single white begonias make an ideal partner for the more flamboyant double white showstopper variety.

BELOW LEFT: Container-grown scented nicotiana and trailing ivy blend seamlessly with other garden plants.

BASIC TECHNIQUES

LOOK FORWARD TO SEASONS OF LUSH CONTAINER DISPLAYS BY INDULGING THEM WITH EVERYTHING THEY NEED FOR THE BEST START. POTS AND COMPOST, PLANTING AND CARE, THIS CHAPTER OUTLINES ALL THE MATERIALS, TOOLS AND TECHNIQUES NEEDED FOR SUCCESSFUL CONTAINER GARDENING.

• CHOOSING CONTAINERS • DECORATING CONTAINERS • TOOLS • POTTING COMPOST
• HOW TO PLANT A CONTAINER • HOW TO PLANT A HANGING BASKET
• HOW TO PLANT BULBS • HOW TO KEEP CONTAINERS LOOKING THEIR BEST

CHOOSING CONTAINERS

As well as the huge range of containers and hanging baskets available in garden centres, there are plenty originally designed for all sorts of other uses that can be adapted for growing plants. Potential candidates need to be at least 15cm (6in) deep to allow for the root development, and they need to have drainage holes (see right), so think laterally about all kinds of containers – not just those designed for the garden. Check out old boxes, baskets or bags; vintage packaging, such as biscuit tins, and fruit and veg boxes, or even recycled kitchen equipment, such as colanders and sieves.

If drainage is already integrated into the design, so much the better, but it is easy to add drainage holes to most containers, such as wood, metal, leather, plastics or even stone. The two materials that do pose a problem are ceramics or glass as it's not possible to drill into them. However, these could be used to hold other planted-up pots that do have drainage holes.

MAKING DRAINAGE HOLES

This is the safe way to make drainage holes in containers. Turn the container upside down and make sure it stands firm without wobbling. Fix a piece of masking tape over the place you would like to drill the hole. The tape will help prevent the drill slipping. Wearing protective gloves, use a hand or electric drill fitted with the appropriate bit (wood, masonry or metal) to make the hole.

Holes can be made in softer materials, such as leather and some plastics, with a sharp skewer, although this should be done using protective gloves.

PREPARING THE POTS

Old pots need to be thoroughly scrubbed out using a stiff scrubbing brush and plenty of running water. The aim is to remove any pests, weeds or diseases. Even if there aren't any evident to the eye, fungal spores, seeds, mites or their eggs may be present.

1 First, brush out the pot using a stiff brush to remove any loose debris and cobwebs.

2 Rinse thoroughly using a fast jet of water. Next, scrub with a solution of garden disinfectant before a final thorough rinse.

3 Turn the pots upside down and allow to drain.

Scrub all containers made from any material in the same way. Wooden containers will also need to be treated from time to time with a plant-friendly timber preservative.

PAINT PROTECTION

If you plan to put containers on a windowsill or any other painted surface, you will need to protect the paintwork as water draining from the compost and becoming trapped under the pots will soon cause the paint to peel. Containers can be put on ordinary kitchen trays, saucers or plates, whilst window boxes will need to sit on special trays made to fit, which are usually available to buy with the window box. Another solution is to sit the container on special feet to raise it off the surface. That way, any moisture from the container can freely drain off the painted surface, minimising any damage.

ABOVE: There is a huge range of containers purpose-made for planting, such as the moss-look urn, top left. Many other items can be adapted for planting, as long as there is drainage, and coffee cups and paper bags can be used as temporary containers for celebration days.

DECORATING
CONTAINERS

The most basic of pots can take on a new lease of life with a little decoration. You don't need to be a great artist or craftsperson – very often the simplest of ideas are the most successful.

Painting the pots is a cheap and easy way to create impact, especially if you want a particular colour scheme. There are also many ways to add simple but elegant design. Geometric designs are best tackled using masking tape. Paint the whole pot in a single colour, then, for example, if you want stripes, add masking tape either in vertical stripes or stripes that go around the pot. Next, paint between the stripes in a contrasting colour. Leave to dry before removing the tape. Simple designs can either be painted on by hand, or you can use stencils (see page 54) or stamps, both of which are easy to do.

The surface of pots can also be embellished using decorative items, such as shells, pebbles, mirror or pieces of broken china, mosaic style. Fix shells and small pebbles using a glue gun and hot wax glue. Mirror, broken china and larger pebbles need to be applied in much the same way as tiles. Use waterproof tile adhesive and grout, designed for bathrooms, so that your work will withstand the weather.

HOW TO PAINT A POT

Brighten up a potted vegetable patch by slipping the plastic pots into inexpensive terracotta, painted for a bright new look. Use two or three colours that can be reversed and interchanged on the pots to give them a co-ordinated look. This simple fish design, painted at intervals around the pot, adds elegant decoration.

New terracotta is easy to paint as it is clean, porous and needs no preparation. Old terracotta will have to be thoroughly cleaned using a solution of washing-up liquid, thoroughly rinsed, given a quick sand, then rinsed again before painting. Plastic pots can be painted if you first paint them with ESP (Easy Surface Preparation). However, this is expensive, so unless you already have some on your DIY shelf, it would probably be cheaper (and less effort) to invest in new terracotta.

1 Wash the pot down and allow it to dry. Paint the pot all over using the exterior paint (to improve weather-proof quality), making sure you cover all the outside surfaces. Allow to dry.

2 Mix a spoonful of blue emulsion into a small quantity of exterior masonry paint to create the shade you want.

3 In the same way, mix up each of the other colours with the exterior masonry paint to the required shades.

4 Turn the pot upside down for stability and paint all over with the mixed main colour. Allow to dry.

5 Turn the pot up the right way again and paint the top edge with a mixed-up colour in a contrasting shade.

6 Using the artist's brush and a contrasting colour, paint a simple fish motif on the pot. Start by painting a dot to mark the tip of the mouth and another to mark the tail. In the same way, mark out the positions of the fish at intervals around the pot. Paint the fish outline.

7 Fill in the body of the fish, then use soft, feathery strokes for the tail. Use light strokes to paint in the fins. Use the main paint colour again to paint in the details of the fish, starting with the eye, then add the gills and finally the long dorsal line.

8 The features of the fish look best if you work fast, and don't worry if each finished fish looks slightly different – this will simply add to the pot's charm.

TOOLS

Container gardeners need only a few small basic tools to get started, none of which need much storage space. Here's a list of the essentials, so gather them together and allocate them a spot in the garden shed where they can be kept together.

SCRUBBING BRUSH

Choose one with firm bristles so you can efficiently scrub out pots before use. This is especially important if you're re-using containers as you need to ensure there are no residual plant diseases, weed seeds, or pests or their eggs that could be passed on to your new planting.

WATERING CAN OR HOSE

Plants need to be watered generously just before they are planted up and again once the container is complete. As you are likely to be using young plants, ensure your watering can or hose has a fine rose attachment so that there is no damage to delicate petals or foliage. Once the containers are planted, watering will be part of your regular regime as a container gardener because they dry out much quicker than flowerbeds.

BUCKET

This is useful for re-hydrating dried-out plants before planting as sometimes the root ball has been allowed to completely dry out. This is a problem, especially with modern soil-less composts, because once they've dried out, they don't easily take up the moisture. The best solution is to plunge the plant, pot and all, into a bucket of water for a few hours until the water has thoroughly soaked through.

A bucket is also useful for releasing the roots of badly pot-bound plants. Although it is best to leave root balls undisturbed, if you do need to peel away a little of the old compost to give more space, instead of doing it by hand which may damage the roots, take the plant out of its pot, then plunge the whole root ball into a bucket of water. Once soaked, you'll find the outside compost comes away easily without damaging even the most delicate roots.

A bucket is also handy when planting hanging baskets. Just sit the basket in the bucket to keep it stable while you get to work.

BELOW: Be careful not to damage the roots of any plants. If you need to loosen a pot-bound root ball, or remove excess compost to make more space in a container, do it by plunging the entire root ball into a bucket of water.

HAND TOOLS

A good hand trowel is essential. Make sure it is strong and the joints are properly welded. Cheaper tools may bend and become misshapen with wear. Also, check that the handle is securely fixed to the metal part of the trowel. Grip it to make sure it's ergonomically suited to your hand and comfortable to use. Some people also like a small fork for surface weeding.

SECATEURS

When planting up, you may need to cut away dead wood, leaves or flowers or even plant labels. Invest in a good-quality pair of secateurs that are sharp enough to make clean cuts, even in woody stems, and thereby promote healthy regrowth. The best for delicate stems are the 'bypass' type, which have double blades like a pair of scissors. 'Anvil' type secateurs have a blade on one side and flat surface to cut against on the other. Some people find these useful when cutting woody stems, but even then, they are unlikely to produce the clean cut of bypass. Again, try before you buy, checking the grip suits your hand.

GARDENING GLOVES

Not necessary, but nice! Gardening gloves provide excellent protection against thorns and help keep your hands clean. Planting containers is not heavy work, so look for some that are not too bulky and fit your hands well. Disposable latex gloves from the pharmacy can be useful, too, keeping your hands clean while you work.

ABOVE: Hand trowels need to be strongly put together and comfortable to use. This is the most useful tool for a container gardener, so make sure you invest in a good-quality one

RIGHT: Hand forks can be useful to help weed the top surface of container plantings.

POTTING COMPOST

The growing medium needs to be bulky enough to support the roots, sterile so that disease and weeds are not passed on, water retentive yet free draining. And it needs to contain enough fertilizer to give the plants a good start. It's a tall order that your garden soil will never live up to. For this reason, it is better to buy compost specially formulated for containers.

This compost falls into two basic categories: soil-based and soil-less. Soil- (or loam-) based composts hold water and fertilizer efficiently, but are inclined to be heavier than their soil-less counterparts, so you may not want to choose them for hanging baskets. Renowned John Innes composts are well-researched loam-based formulae that manufacturers follow for certain applications. Choose John Innes No. 2 for summer baskets; No. 3 for longer-term containers.

Soil-less composts are generally lighter and cleaner to use. However, many are peat-based, contributing to the ecologically unfriendly reduction of the world's peat bogs. If you'd prefer to use non-peat compost, look for some that is coir-based, made from coconut waste.

There are also composts of both kinds specially formulated for bulbs (bulb fibre). It's not essential you use these, though they include oyster shell and wood charcoal to keep the compost fresh over the winter and microbes to combat mould and disease.

Lime-hating plants, such as rhododendrons and heathers, must be planted in ericaceous compost if they are to flourish.

If you don't use up the whole sack of any compost, make sure it is well sealed before storing to stop it from drying out or pests from getting in.

EXTRA HELP

By their very nature, containers limit the amount of water and nutrients available to plants, so it's a good idea to give them a little help by adding in a few extras when planting up.

Water-retaining granules Also known as moisture-retaining gel, these granules can hold up to 400 times their own weight in water, which can help keep the compost wet between waterings. All you need to add is a teaspoon or two, depending on the size of the container and product supplier. Always follow the manufacturer's recommendations.

Slow-release fertilizers Slow-release fertilizers are another invaluable addition. They are made up of balls of water-soluble nutrients, which dissolve into the compost over

time. Temperature sensitive, they release more nutrients during the growing months as the weather gets warmer. They often come with a special measuring spoon so you can easily work out the quantity per litre of compost. Slow-release nutrients should last up to six months, although you can always add extra liquid feed towards the end of this time.

Perlite This is a volcanic material that has been 'popped' like popcorn over high heat to create a growing medium supplement. It improves moisture retention and lightens and aerates the soil, making moisture and nutrients more readily available to the plants. The usual recommendation for containers is to mix one part perlite with two parts compost. Perlite is extremely light, weighing about a quarter of the equivalent volume of wet loam. It is useful if you have larger containers where you want to keep the weight down, such as when used on rooftop gardens.

Sharp sand Plants such as succulents that need free drainage could suffer from rot if planted in ordinary proprietary container compost. However, you can easily improve the drainage by mixing in lime-free washed sharp sand in the proportions of three parts loam-based compost to one part sand. Readily available from garden centres, make sure you always ask for horticultural grade sand.

MULCH

Anything that covers and protects the surface of the compost is a mulch. The main function of mulch, as far as containers are concerned, is to help retain moisture and reduce weed growth, whilst adding a decorative touch. There are plenty to choose from, such as coloured glass, pebbles of various sizes, coloured gravels and small shells, available in garden centres and DIY stores. You can also improvise with interesting alternatives, such as old champagne or wine corks, conkers or acorns. Choose the mulch either to complement the container or the hues of the flowers to create more colour impact and a smart finished look.

Natural beach cobbles and pebbles have a rounded appearance, and come in various sizes and colours ranging from almost pure white to very dark charcoal with a wide selection of natural tones in between. The sizes range from boulders, which are the largest at 600mm (2ft) and not really suitable for containers, to the smallest pebbles at around 20mm (¾in). Most cobbles range from 50–200mm (2–8in) and make a smart mulch for larger pots. Gravel, which is made up of much smaller chips of stone, comes in various colours, some of which incorporate a natural sparkle. Paddlestones are another natural product. They are supplied as a mixture of differently sized pieces of slate that range from little-finger size to pieces up to 10cm (4in) across. They are tumbled to soften their edges. Polished pebbles and agates have an elegant, shiny look, and come in a range of natural colours from almost black to white with amber and amethyst tones in between.

RIGHT: Polished stone mulches come in a surprising range of colours. These amethyst-toned stones make a perfect combination with bugle (*Ajuga reptans* 'Atropurpurea').

RIGHT: The soft natural tones of shells can make a charming mulch, but you need to ensure they're ecologically collected. Ask your fishmonger for cockle shells (like these) or mussel shells — both display a delightful range of colours that work well with plants.

HOW TO PLANT A CONTAINER

When planting a container, the aim is to create a rich splash of colour in a limited space. This often means packing the plants in a little tighter than you would in the borders. Container plants are limited in their access to nutrients and water, so you need to mix these into the compost.

These steps show the method for planting a container. The ideas in this book are based on this technique, except they also include the names and quantities of the plants needed for that particular planting. When creating your own ideas for plantings, follow these instructions.

LEFT: Soft coral shades of petunias and million bells perfectly complement the dusky tones of a Cretan terracotta container. By the end of the summer, these plants will be tumbling voluptuously over the side of the pot.

1 Thoroughly scrub out the pots (see page 10). Water the plants and allow to drain. If they have been allowed to dry out, plunge the plants, including their pots, into a bucket of water for a few hours to re-hydrate, then allow to drain.

2 Place some crocks (such as broken china, large stones or a piece of slate) or gravel at the bottom of the pot to cover the drainage hole. This will provide better drainage and also prevent the compost falling through the hole.

3 Mix water-retaining granules (see page 16) with potting compost in the proportions recommended by the manufacturer (read the notes on the packaging).

4 Also mix slow-release fertilizer into the compost to the proportions set out by the manufacturer.

5 Ensure that the prepared compost reaches an appropriate level in the pot for the largest plant.

6 Try out the plants for the best arrangement. Take their growing habits into consideration. Put the tallest plants towards the back and trailing ones at the outer edges of the container.

7 Remove the largest plant from its pot, being careful not to damage its roots and place in the container. Add the other plants. You need to allow at least 2.5cm (1in) space between and around each plant, which will eventually be filled with compost.

8 Carefully fill between and around the plants with compost, pressing it down firmly with your fingers. Finish with a layer of mulch (see page 17) to help prevent the pot drying out.

9 Finally, thoroughly water the container until the water runs out of the bottom of the pot.

HOW TO PLANT A HANGING BASKET

Wonderful tumbling blooms hoisted high to eye level must be one of the most glorious hallmarks of summer gardens. Plant them up in springtime to allow them to really develop their roots so they can send out a lush show throughout the summer.

Planting up a hanging basket is not much different to planting up any container, except that you need to bear in mind that the underside will be seen, especially early on when the plants are small and newly bedded in. The tactics are to use a green liner or to camouflage it with moss, and to grow some of the plants through the sides of the basket. If you're not using a traditional wire hanging basket, opting for a solid one instead (such as the cornucopia on page 106), this will not be a problem. You could also try recycling a container to use for a hanging basket, such as an old shopping basket or a pretty plastic Chinese shopping bag. Or you may even decide to hang up an old colander.

SUPPORTING THE BASKET

Whatever container you choose, make sure it will be able to support its contents once it is filled with compost and plants, bearing in mind that water contributes to extra weight. This is particularly pertinent if you're using a recycled basket, for example, which may break under the strain.

You'll also need to make sure that any hooks, brackets or branches that you plan to hang the basket from, plus the chains or ropes by which you plan to hang them, are strong and firmly fixed. Once hung up, you just need to keep the baskets well watered and deadheaded.

ABOVE: Even a basket simply made up of a selection of pansies plus pretty variegated trailing ivy can bring a fabulous splash of colour to a focal point in the garden.

HANGING BASKET LINERS

Most traditional hanging baskets need a liner to contain the compost and retain the water. These also have a decorative function as they will be on show when the basket is newly planted up and until the plants have filled out.

Cardboard These are usually made from recycled paper and coloured green. Most are made to fit particular basket sizes. Some people add a little moss between basket and liner to improve the aesthetics.

Coconut fibre Eco-friendly, being made from natural waste, the most aesthetically pleasing fibre liners are stained green. Can be cut to size.

1 Collect all the ingredients together and thoroughly water all the plants.

2 Sit the basket on a bucket for support. Prepare the liner, cutting it down to size, if necessary, using a pair of scissors.

3 Fill the bottom of the basket with soil-less compost to about halfway up the sides of the basket liner. This compost is generally lighter than soil-based compost, and so the best choice for hanging baskets.

4 Mix some water-retaining granules (see page 16) into the compost, following the proportions recommended by the manufacturer.

5 Add some slow-release fertilizer (see page 16) to the basket, also following the proportions recommended by the manufacturer.

6 Start by planting into the side of the basket, either where there are slits already in the liner, or cut some extra slits using scissors. Ivy, or similar plants, can be fed through roots first from the outside.

7 In the same way, plant some blue pansies into the side of the basket. If the root ball is too big, wrap the plant in a piece of thin plastic and feed that through the side of the hanging basket from the inside. The plastic will protect the flowers and leaves, and keep them neatly together while you do this. Once it is through, simply remove the plastic.

8 Also plant some magenta and yellow pansies around the sides. Add another layer of compost to almost fill the basket, then arrange the remainder of the plants in the top. Fill around and between the plants with more compost and press in firmly with your fingers. Water well until the water runs through the bottom of the basket, then hang the basket.

HOW TO PLANT BULBS

Early autumn is the time to plant up spring bulbs. Plan for a long flowering period by planting them up in layers, then look forward to a succession of blooms through the spring. Top the container with autumn interest to keep it decorative while you're waiting for the bulbs to appear.

The general rule for planting bulbs is to plant them at a depth twice the size of the bulb, pointed end upwards. The bulb planting shown below consists of crocuses, which are one of the first bulbs to appear at the end of winter, then the daffodils in early spring, followed by tulips in late spring.

In the garden, bulb leaves should be left on for as long as possible, as the sunlight helps to replenish the bulb, ready for next year's growth. Keep to this principle as far as possible for container plants. This should not be a problem when daffodils follow crocuses as they are so much larger and their leaves will soon cover the smaller crocus leaves. However, when the daffodils are past their best, their leaves can look messy and are unlikely to be fully covered by the tulip leaves. You can either cut them down if you feel they have just become far too unruly, or neaten them by plaiting them together, or tying them up with raffia to make a feature of them amongst the tulips.

USING BULB FIBRE

When planting bulbs, many people choose bulb fibre, which includes oyster shell and wood charcoal to keep the compost fresh over the winter and microbes to combat mould and disease. You won't need water-retaining granules because damp winter and spring conditions mean that containers kept outside are unlikely to dry out. You can dispense with slow-release fertilizers, too, as bulbs themselves are a natural goody store that gives the plant all it needs to make its astonishing spring growth spurt.

1 Scrub out a container at least 40cm (16in) deep. Add a layer of crocks to the bottom to improve drainage.

2 Put some bulb fibre compost into the bottom of the container. Add a layer of tulip bulbs. The tighter you pack them, the better the display, so arrange them so the bulbs almost touch each other. They need to be planted at a depth twice the size of the bulb.

3 Add a thin layer of bulb fibre over the tulips, but keep the tips still showing. Position a layer of daffodil bulbs, allowing enough space for the tips of the tulips to grow up between them.

4 Add more bulb fibre to bring the level up to the correct planting level for crocuses, which is twice the size of the bulb. In the same way, position the crocus bulbs in the container.

ABOVE AND RIGHT: The astonishing energy with which spring bulbs seem to push up through bare earth, bursting into flamboyant, colourful blooms, is so welcome after months of dark winter bleakness. This makes all the early autumn effort of planting them up well worthwhile.

5 Finish planting, add more compost, then either add a mulch or dress the top with a leafy plant. Water well. Leave outside in winter where there should be adequate rain and natural moisture to keep the compost damp. Check occasionally to ensure the container doesn't dry out.

HOW TO KEEP CONTAINERS LOOKING THEIR BEST

ABOVE: Many bedding plants, including petunias, need regular deadheading to keep the blooms coming throughout the summer. Simply pull out the dead blooms with your fingers.

ABOVE RIGHT: Tall, slender cosmos should be regularly deadheaded. As summer progresses, you may need to stake the plants for support.

BELOW RIGHT: The underplanted pansies will need deadheading, but leave the large agapanthus blooms to go to seed in the autumn. Their large seedheads make a striking autumn and winter display.

FAR RIGHT: Iceland poppies should be deadheaded, but it's good to leave a few seedheads to develop to give variety.

Careful planting gives containers an excellent start, but they need some tender loving care to keep them looking good. Keep them regularly watered, which could mean every day in the hottest months. Early morning or around dusk is the best time as you risk scorching the leaves if you water them when the sun is shining.

Regular deadheading helps to keep some flowers blooming and encourages more growth – check the plant labels. As the plants grow, so they produce ever more blooms, so this could also be a daily task.

DEALING WITH PESTS

While deadheading, check for pests. The best way to get rid of greenfly is to squash them between your fingers. Alternatively, spray them with a proprietary bug killer. Slugs and snails can devastate some plants. Discourage them by using gritty mulches, which they hate to cross, and surround the pot in grit. Proprietary slug killers can be a last option – choose a child- and pet-friendly one.

WATERING CONTAINERS

One of the greatest conundrums of summer containers is what to do when you go on holiday. If you have a green-fingered neighbour, you could swap watering chores. If not, consider putting in a simple irrigation system. You can buy kits for the precision irrigation of containers. They usually consist of microbore feed pipes, drippers and a battery-controlled timer to ensure containers are each delivered their own supply, whilst using minimum water. By timing the irrigation to come on for just a few minutes in the night, you can make most efficient use of the water, avoiding any evaporation. The system can be fitted to a garden tap or, for water conservation, to a water butt.

JUNK GENIUS JUNK CAN BE
SURPRISINGLY GORGEOUS, SO RESCUE THE BEST BEFORE IT EVEN
HITS THE RECYCLING BIN. LOOK OUT FOR PLASTIC BOTTLES, WIRE
OR WICKER BASKETS, METAL BOXES AND GALVANIZED WATERING
CANS – THEY CAN ALL MAKE PERFECT HOMES FOR YOUR PLANTS.

• A BOTTLE OF BLOOMS • CANNED COLOUR • SUMMER BASKET
• CAGED UP • OLD-TIME BLUES • METAL GURUS

A BOTTLE OF BLOOMS

Plastic water bottles make great junk containers because many come with pretty labels with interesting graphics and they're easily adapted to create perfect summer containers. Gather together several of the same design for impact. Alternatively, make up a collection of bottles in a mixture of shapes and sizes with contrasting labels. Simply cut off the tops and plant up the bottles with the best of the season's bedding. Giveaway containers like these can be used with abandon. For example, you could line them up along the length of a buffet table, team a trio on a tray for decorative interest on the garden table, or pot up a posse for impact on the patio.

AFTERCARE

Needs full sun for half the day, regular watering and regular feeding. Deadhead for blooming right up until the first autumn frosts.

YOU WILL NEED

An empty plastic water bottle
Bradawl, gimlet or other pointed instrument
Hacksaw
Scissors

Gravel
Potting compost
Calibrachoa Million Bells (this is often referred to incorrectly as a petunia)

1 Thoroughly water the plant and allow to drain. Using the bradawl, pierce the bottom of the bottle to make a drainage hole. Using the hacksaw, make a cut across the neck of the bottle, then insert the scissors and cut off the top.

2 Place a handful of gravel into the bottom of the bottle to provide efficient drainage. Add a layer of potting compost.

3 Tip the Million Bells upside down to release from the pot, then place in the bottle, taking care not to damage the roots.

4 Carefully fill the space between the plant and sides of the bottle with compost and press down firmly with your fingers. Finish with a top layer of compost. Water thoroughly.

CANNED COLOUR

Transform packaging tins into colourful plant-friendly containers simply by drilling drainage holes into their bases. It's a favourite trick in Mediterranean countries where olive oil, biscotti and amaretti are often sold in decorative tins adorned with great graphics. Follow their lead by scouring Italian delicatessens and other ethnic food stores, such as Turkish, Spanish and Asian, for suitable containers. Even regular supermarkets can be great hunting grounds, especially at Christmas time when luxury treats, such as special biscuit and chocolate collections, are often sold in decorative tins.

The safest way to make the holes in the tins is to turn the tin upside down and stick masking tape on the base where you want to make the hole. This stops the screwdriver or drill bit you're using to make the hole from slipping. Make several holes to allow for adequate drainage.

You can plant up a single container, co-ordinating it with the colour of the plants; or you can be a little more flamboyant, mixing colours and styles. The extrovert nature of most of these tin designs means you can group them with abandon, making a collection that grows over the years.

AFTERCARE

Both the gaillardia and pansies shown here appreciate a sunny, well-drained position and regular watering. Gaillardias can be planted in spring, and will reward you with non-stop flowers from spring until early autumn, provided you deadhead them frequently. There's a choice of pansies (*Viola* x *wittrockiana*) available during both summer and winter which will reward you with continuous flowering if regularly deadheaded.

TOP LEFT: Flirty pansy 'Frizzle Sizzle Yellow Blue Swirl' combines both sunny yellow and cool blue tones in a biscuit tin.

CENTRE LEFT: Rich purple pansies perfectly complement the soft tones of a tall amaretti tin.

BOTTOM LEFT: An orange biscotti tin is home to a vibrant gaillardia and deep purple pansies with yellow centres.

RIGHT: The extrovert hues of traditional Mediterranean biscuit tins make fabulous summer containers, especially when planted with co-ordinating bedding in full bloom.

SUMMER BASKET

Rescued from cellars, attics or junk stalls, old baskets make delightful summer containers for decks, patios or windowsills. Suspended by rope from wall brackets, or even from tree branches, they can also make great hanging containers, though do check old basketwork is strong enough to take the weight of its watered contents before hoisting it up high.

Aged basketwork has a cottage feel, so keep it in character with a pretty country-style planting scheme. This basketful of yellows and pinks is planted with simple cottage-garden flowers that have disarming children's colouring-book charm. It makes a delightful summer splash that blooms right through until the beginning of autumn.

If your style is somewhat more funky, search out inexpensive plastic shopping baskets in bright colours and plant them up with blooms in lively, clashing hues.

AFTERCARE

Place in a sunny position and keep moist. Deadhead regularly for an abundance of blooms all summer.

YOU WILL NEED

Basket
Plastic, for lining basket
Scissors
Trowel
Gravel, to aid drainage
Slow-release fertilizer
Moisture-retaining granules
Container compost

6 marigolds (*Calendula*)
3 *Zinnia* 'Profusion Cherry'
3 black-eyed Susan (*Thunbergia alata* 'Yellow Star')
Garden twine

ABOVE: Collect all the ingredients together and make sure the plants are thoroughly watered before beginning the planting.

RIGHT: As the summer progresses, all the plants will put on a surprising amount of growth, tumbling over the sides of the basket.

1 Water the plants well and allow to drain. Cut a piece of plastic to create a lining for the base and sides of the basket.

2 Using a pair of scissors, cut slits in several places in the plastic at the bottom of the basket to ensure good drainage.

3 Using a trowel, add a layer of gravel to the bottom of the basket. This provides excellent drainage, ensuring the plants don't get waterlogged. Mix fertilizer and moisture-retaining granules, according to manufacturer's instructions, into enough compost to fill the basket.

4 Position the marigolds and zinnias in the basket, making an attractive arrangement. Give each plant a little space, bearing in mind they'll thicken up over the course of the summer.

5 The black-eyed Susan will be sold supported on a cane. Carefully tip the pot up to remove the plant while retaining the cane. Add to the basket. Fill any gaps between plants with more compost.

6 Using garden twine, tie some black-eyed Susan to the top of the cane and allow others to trail over the edge of the basket, making a pleasing shape overall. Water well.

BELOW: Pot marigolds (*Calendula*) are a traditional cottage favourite. They produce generous flushes of sunny blooms, ranging from cream through yellow to orange, from spring to autumn.

CAGED UP

Plants don't always have to keep just their roots in containers. Given a wire basket, or even an old birdcage, both of which allow plenty of through-light, there's no reason why the whole plant can't be contained. The overall effect gives the impression of a transparent screening with a layer-upon-layer look. So scour junk markets and charity shops for cages of all kinds – both ornamental and the vacated homes of our feathered friends – for suitable containers.

Placing the entire pot into the 'cage' can pose a problem with some birdcages that have very small openings, so look out for those with more generous doors. The pots themselves can be either disguised by a mulch of pebbles, shells or stones (as seen here), or wrapped in a piece of waterproof fabric to make them look more attractive.

AFTERCARE

Helichrysum petiolare and trailing ivy have been used here. These two easy-grow evergreens both like full sun or partial shade. Water regularly to avoid drying out.

ABOVE: A simple wirework basket hung on a bough brings greenery high up where it's needed. This one has been filled with a froth of *Helichrysum petiolare* 'Yellow' and trailing ivy. Their pots have been concealed in Scottish cobble mulch.

LEFT: Over the summer the *Helichrysum* will grow through the wire, making a luscious froth of green, perfect for hanging from brackets or branches to disguise any bare sections of fence or wall.

OLD-TIME BLUES

Unlike store-bought goods, the ranks of recycled, restored and salvaged don't come co-ordinated, but this simply offers you plenty of scope for you to build your own 'team'. Here, a wire garden basket has found a visual friend in an old enamelled herb box. Their common material (metal) provides the link; a bond that has been strengthened by using predominantly purple planting.

Both containers have unsophisticated cottage charm, so they've been filled with cottage-style plants. Delightful meadow-like scabious (*Scabiosa lucida*) teamed with pretty purple-veined ornamental cabbage (*Brassica oleracea*) give the sense of a pottage garden where decorative blooms traditionally cosied up with produce. The scabious will merrily flower all summer, provided you deadhead regularly, and the cabbage will fill out into luscious purple-veined foliage. Both make great pickings for the flower arranger, so don't hold back: cut them to enjoy indoors, too.

YOU WILL NEED
2 ornamental cabbage (*Brassica oleracea*)
Heavy-duty scissors
Hanging basket liner
Wire basket
Water-retaining granules
Slow-release fertilizer
Potting compost
Scottish cobbles

1 Thoroughly water all the plants, then allow to drain. If they have previously dried out, plunge them into a bucket of water for at least an hour before planting up.

2 Using heavy-duty scissors, cut the hanging basket liner to fit the contours of the wire basket. The liner needs to cover the base and the lower part of the sides.

3 Place the liner in the basket, smoothing it out with your hands. Mix water-retaining granules and fertilizer, following the manufacturer's instructions, into enough compost to fill the container. Place a layer of this mixed compost into the bottom of the basket.

ABOVE: The soft grey-green tones of both plants and containers make a pleasing colour combination.

RIGHT: You don't have to put plant combinations all in one container: linking them with a colour theme, then grouping them together can be just as successful. Here, cottage-garden scabious in a herb tin teams well with the allotment-style cabbages in an old wire garden basket. The combination harks back to traditional pottage gardens that combined produce and flowers.

4 Carefully remove the cabbages from their pots and place at either end of the basket, allowing plenty of space all around for them to grow and fill out.

5 Add more mixed compost all around the cabbage plants, making sure the entire root balls are well covered.

6 Gently pat the compost down between the plants, ensuring they are held in place securely.

7 Use Scottish cobbles or similar as a mulch around the cabbages to cover the compost. As the cabbages grow, you may want to remove some or all of the stones. Thoroughly water the basket.

AFTERCARE

Position in a sunny spot or partial shade. Water well when the surface compost feels dry to the touch. Do not allow the compost to dry out. The main enemy is the cabbage white butterfly which likes to lay its eggs on the cabbage, providing a feast for its caterpillars. Check regularly for eggs and remove them immediately, not forgetting the underside of the leaves.

LEFT: The colours of this antique enamel container work well with the soft tones of scabious (*Scabiosa lucida*). Make a hole in the bottom of the tin container using a bradawl and hammer (see page 40). Keep the scabious well watered and deadhead them regularly, and you'll be rewarded with flowers for much of the summer.

OPPOSITE, TOP LEFT: The frilly blue petals of the scabious lend the appearance of layers of pretty petticoats.

TOP RIGHT: The luminous lavender-blue tones have timeless appeal.

OPPOSITE, BOTTOM LEFT: Soft grey cobbles make the perfect mulch for the cabbages. As the plants grow, give them space by taking out some of the cobbles.

BOTTOM RIGHT: Nature's colour schemes are always the most inspired, as demonstrated by the vibrant purple veins running through the blue-green cabbage leaves.

METAL GURUS

There are plenty of pickings when it comes to recycled metal, partly because its resilience means that much of it survives the wear and tear of its original purpose (and even after that, while loitering in attics, garden sheds, even builders' skips). Galvanized metal often improves with age, its original bright shiny looks replaced by a soft bloom, whilst copper metamorphoses from its familiar burnished tones to a subtle green. Look out, too, for decorative wrought iron, shiny tin and, for a more modern look, discarded zinc or stainless steel containers.

As well as being easy to source, metal makes an excellent plant container because it's both tough and waterproof. However, before it can be used, you need to make at least one drainage hole in the bottom. Do this by turning it upside down and placing a piece of masking tape where you would like the drainage hole to appear (the tape prevents the drill or tool slipping). Using a drill or bradawl and hammer, carefully make a hole or two.

ABOVE: Metal watering cans which are past their prime can enjoy a successful reincarnation as plant containers in cottage-style gardens.

LEFT: Given a lick of weatherproof paint, even old dustbins can make smart containers either side of the front door. Planted with grasses and ivy, these are easy to maintain will look good all year round. Keep watered but well drained. Cut out any dead grasses and leaves.

RIGHT: A trio of watering cans used as containers makes a delightful garden feature. It works best if you use varying sizes and co-ordinate the planting. The combination of the blue-green leaves of the *Euphorbia myrsinites*, the pinks (*Dianthus* 'Pink Jewel') and pretty purple pansies (*Viola* x *wittrockiana*), make a delightful summer group. Keep all the plants moist and deadhead the flowers. At the end of the summer, replace the pansies with winter-flowering equivalents (the euphorbia and pinks are evergreen).

LOCATION, LOCATION

POSITION POTS CAREFULLY FOR FOCUS IN THE GARDEN.
LET THEM BRING ADDED INTEREST TO DOORWAYS, WINDOWS AND
SEATING OR EATING AREAS, LEND IMPORTANCE TO PATHWAYS AND
ENTRANCES, OR MAKE A BOLD STATEMENT ON THE DECK.

• SUMMER BLUES • GREEN GODDESS • PERFUMED PURPLE • PATHWAY POINTERS
• FRONT FEATURES • DOOR STOPPERS • FURNITURE FOCUS

SUMMER BLUES

Large pots and urns which provide a permanent sculptural element in the garden are not always easy to move, but that doesn't mean you have to be limited to a single look. One solution is to plant up plastic containers that can fit inside the permanent ones, and as the year progresses, swap in alternative combinations. The photos here and on pages 45–49 all feature the same container, demonstrating how you can change the look throughout the seasons. In order to raise the inner pot to the correct level, it's a good idea to place an upturned flowerpot inside the 'host' container, to support the planted-up plastic pot.

In summer, this antique Cretan urn is planted up with classic bedding, which fills out into lush colour tumbling down the sides of the pot. Ideally, these plants should be planted up by the middle of spring to give them time to get their roots really established for the lushest summer colour. However, one option is for the newly planted-up young plants to be allowed to grow on in a quiet part of the garden for a couple of weeks, allowing them to

ABOVE: *Petunia* Surfinia Blue produces continuous blooms all summer and through into early autumn, while morning glories have a pretty trailing habit with flowers that look like the petunias' dainty cousins. White petunias lend contrast to the combination.

thicken up a little before being placed inside the Cretan container for the summer.

The combination of blue and white is a delightfully fresh summer favourite. It is always successful and easy to put together, choosing from a wide selection of bedding plants in those hues. This planting is made up from *Petunia* Surfinia in white and blue, teamed with dainty morning glories (*Ipomoea hederacea*). They all have a charming trailing habit, while the petunias have a bushiness that also lends height to the planting. Petunias and morning glories are an ever-popular summer planting because they provide a mass of blooms all through the season, right into early autumn.

AFTERCARE

Keep the container well watered, never letting it dry out. Deadhead regularly – as the summer progresses and the plants put on growth, this will become a daily exercise.

GREEN GODDESS

Feather-like ferns make a glorious green statement in containers. Ranging from light, bright lettuce-green shades through rich emeralds and silver, there's a wide choice of tones to suit every situation. Their elegant fronds stretch upwards and outwards in a delightful habit. Better still, many are evergreen and thus can brighten darker winter days.

This fern was planted up in late summer with winter pansies (*Viola* x *wittrockiana* 'Rose Blotch') for floral interest through the autumn and into the winter. Pretty variegated trailing ivy adds lower interest to the planter, softening the contours of the container. Within a couple of weeks the pansies will thicken out, bringing more colour to the whole ensemble, while the ivy will fill out over the course of the winter.

AFTERCARE

Keep the pot watered but well drained. Deadhead the pansies daily, as needed.

YOU WILL NEED

1 large fern, ideally evergreen
6 pansies (*Viola* x *wittrockiana* 'Rose Blotch')
3 variegated ivy plants
Drainage stone or crock
1 container with a diameter no larger than that of the 'host' container, plus a spare pot (see page 44)
Water-retaining granules
Slow-release fertilizer
Compost
Trowel

ABOVE: Pretty feathery ferns lend an architectural feel to the containers. Choose an evergreen variety for all year interest, then add pansies for their colour.

1 Collect together all the 'ingredients' and thoroughly soak the plants and their compost with water. Leave to stand for at least half an hour to allow the water to soak into the compost and drain through.

2 Place a crock or stone over the drainage hole in the pot. Mix the water-retaining granules and fertilizer, following the manufacturer's instructions, into a measure of compost that would fill the container. Trowel some compost into the bottom of the container.

3 Carefully release the fern from its pot and lower into the container. Add more compost around the base of the fern's root ball to bring it up to a level appropriate for the pansies.

4 Carefully break the polystyrene strip off the young pansy plants, taking care not to damage their tender roots.

5 Arrange the pansies around the fern. Within a couple of weeks, these will thicken up, providing more seasonal colour.

6 Release the ivies from their pots and add to the container, spacing them equally between the pansies. Carefully add compost to fill gaps between each plant, pressing it down firmly with your fingers.

7 Once the container is planted up, water copiously and allow to drain through. Lower this carefully into the permanent container, making sure it's well supported underneath by the spare upturned pot.

LEFT: The rich raspberry tones of pansy 'Rose Blotch' lend colour to the planting through the winter.

RIGHT: Ferns, variegated ivy and pansies make a refreshing winter planting.

BELOW: Choose a fern in a lime-green shade for a lively, sparkling look.

PERFUMED PURPLE

The best plantings are more than just a visual joy – the addition of a heady scent simply adds to the sensory experience and that is just one secret of success here. Purple stocks (*Matthiola* 'Harmony') add both perfume and colour to a combination that includes *Verbena rigida* and pretty little pansies. It works because the verbena lends structure to the planting, whilst the stocks and pansies bring intense colour saturation. They also all bloom generously all summer, filling out and becoming even more colourful as the season progresses – a wonderful patio or deck combination, especially if that's where you sit or eat, as you can appreciate the natural heady perfume of the stocks. These have been planted up in a separate pot that is then placed inside the Cretan containers, resident on the generous ship-like deck.

AFTERCARE

Keep watered. Deadhead pansies and cut stock blooms when past their best. All plants will flower through the summer, with the pansies and verbena continuing through until autumn.

ABOVE: Pansies come in a wide range of shades. Choose one that adds intensity to the other colours in the container.

RIGHT AND FAR RIGHT: The rigid growing habit of the verbena lends shape and structure to the container, whilst the stocks punch in blocks of strong colour.

BELOW RIGHT: Stocks have the most wonderful scent, particularly noticeable on still summer evenings.

YOU WILL NEED

1 container with a diameter no larger than that of the 'host' container, plus a spare pot (see page 44)

Drainage crock or pebble

2 *Verbena rigida*

4 stocks (*Matthiola* 'Harmony')

6 pansies (*Viola* x *wittrockiana*)

Compost

Water-retaining granules

Slow-release fertilizer

1 Collect together all the ingredients. Thoroughly water all the plants and allow to drain. Place a crock or pebble over the drainage hole in the container.

2 Make up a quantity of compost with added water-retaining granules and fertilizer, according to the manufacturer's instructions, to half-fill the container and place a layer in the bottom. Remove the verbenas from their pots and plant in the container.

3 Add a little compost around the verbenas to bring it up to an appropriate level to accommodate the stocks and pansies. Add the stocks.

4 Carefully tip the pansies out of their pots, making sure you don't damage their delicate roots. Place these between the stocks

5 Fill in and around the plants with the remaining compost, pressing it between the plants with your fingers. Finish with a light top layer. Water well, then place the pot inside the Cretan urn.

PATHWAY POINTERS

Pots positioned with flair lend a greater sense of importance to even the simplest of pathways and this, in turn, can enhance the overall landscaping. Let a pair of planters 'announce' the beginning of a pathway, or a generously proportioned urn provide a focus at the end of a walkway. Alternatively, place a striking container filled with a fabulous combination of plants to provide a spotlight where pathways cross.

The containers themselves add an architectural element to the garden, providing a link between landscaping and planting. They also provide an excellent opportunity to ring the changes. You may use smart low containers one year for an open look, and replace them next season with taller containers (or display the low ones on pedestals) for a gateway feel with a sense of mystery beyond. As well as pathways, you can mark steps with containers, adding a vertical element to the garden.

ABOVE AND BELOW: Here, smart, square white planters, generously filled with heavenly night-scented *Nicotiana alata* and trailing variegated ivy, mark the beginning of the pathway. This not only signals a change of pace in the garden, but offers up a heady fragrance at dusk, inviting relaxing, unwinding evening strolls through the garden. *Nicotiana alata* prefers a sunny spot. Water well and deadhead frequently.

ABOVE AND ABOVE LEFT: A tall chimney-style terracotta container filled with orange and yellow nasturtiums (*Tropaeolum majus*) makes a glorious statement in the circus formed where two paths cross. Climbing up bamboo supports and trailing down towards the ground, these flamboyant blooms make an ever-more striking focus as the summer progresses. Keep watered during the flowering period and deadhead regularly for enthusiastic blooming throughout the summer into early autumn.

LEFT: Extrovert *Gaillardia* 'Fanfare' planted in biscotti tins and spicy green chillies in amaretti tins stride up garden steps, offering vertical interest from late spring right through to the end of summer. Gaillardias appreciate a sunny, well-drained position teamed with regular watering.

FRONT FEATURES

If ever first impressions count, when it comes to your home the front door has to take priority. While many people grow pretty but predictable wisterias or roses upfront, or opt for something more city-smart, like clipped box or bay, the owners of this house have dressed up the front with a lush potted jungle. Garden-loving city-dwellers, they were not prepared to go without plants simply because conservation regulations in the area in which they live prevent them from damaging the paving that extends right up to their threshold. So they contained the lot! (One added benefit is that when it comes to redecorating the front of the house, all the pots can simply be moved to one side.)

Although this planting scheme has taken a few years to reach maturity, it demonstrates the extraordinary abundance that can be achieved by a container garden. This is no one-season wonder: most of the plants are evergreen, giving the house more than simply a rich, extrovert front elevation, but all the ecological benefits of living with plants all year round.

AFTERCARE

The bamboo will need plenty of water to put on lush growth. Keep the other plants watered, too, but they like to be well drained and their roots will not appreciate being waterlogged.

TOP LEFT: White agapanthus positively thrives from being pot bound, and typically, the tighter the roots, the more it blooms. Enjoy these generous flowers all summer, and look forward to large, architectural-looking seedheads in the autumn. The leaves remain green all year, though by the end of the winter you'll need to remove those that have yellowed. In summer, keep it watered but well drained.

LEFT: This pretty little mews house originally had stabling at ground level, which means there are no ground-floor windows, only a door, giving the owners plenty of jungle-growing scope.

RIGHT: Bamboo, the large *Euphorbia mellifera* with umbrella-like leaves growing in front of it, and the agapanthus are all evergreen. *Acanthus mollis* is semi-evergreen, producing the stately bear's breeches spire-like bloom to the right of the picture.

DOOR STOPPERS

Celebrate autumn at the front door by planting up some baby trees with leaves that showcase stunning seasonal colour. This group (pictured right) looks spectacular, set off by the extrovert lime-green blooms of *Hydrangea arborescens* 'Annabelle' planted in the border behind, which blooms throughout the summer and early autumn.

The owner of this house has added a witty and practical touch to this planting by stencilling the house number on the front of one of the terracotta pots. It's a simple idea with a personal touch that's easy to copy. The large, clear house number will always be appreciated by visitors and delivery people alike, especially if it can be seen from the end of the path or drive. However, you can easily adapt the idea by applying more elaborate stencils in different patterns from the wide range of ready-cuts available in craft and decorating stores.

AFTERCARE

Place in a sheltered position so autumn winds don't blow the leaves off prematurely. Keep all plants watered and do not allow to dry out.

YOU WILL NEED

1 terracotta pot with a fairly flat surface

Pre-cut stencil

Masking or gaffer tape

Stencil brush (one that has short, stiff bristles, all cut to the same length)

Stencil paint (paint which has a naturally thick consistency)

Scrap paper

Sand paper

1 Carefully stick the stencil into position on the container using gaffer tape or masking tape, ensuring the number is flat against the pot. This needs special attention, especially if the pot is curved.

2 Using a stencil brush, dip just the very ends into the stencil paint. Dab the brush several times on scrap paper to work off any excess paint and to distribute it evenly amongst the bristles. Holding the brush at right angles to the surface of the pot, 'stipple' the paint on in a dabbing motion.

3 Leave for about an hour to ensure the paint is completely dry before removing the stencil paper.

RIGHT: The *Berberis thunbergii* f. *atropurpurea* (in the numbered pot), which grows to about 2m (6ft), will be happily contained for a few years, providing plenty of interest throughout much of the year: its brilliant orange-red autumn leaves will drop in winter, soon to be replaced by pale green spring leaves and pale yellow flowers, followed by bright red fruits in the summer. The sweet gum (*Liquidambar styraciflua*) in the pot behind brings striking autumn focus to the front door, but you may prefer to plant it into the ground after one season as it can to grow to 20m high x 12m spread (65ft x 40ft).

BELOW LEFT: Twigs laid on top of the compost make an unusual mulch for this berberis.

BELOW RIGHT: Pretty little pine cones make a delightful seasonal mulch and add interest to the pot.

4 The clear simplicity of stencilled numbers is their charm. If for any reason some paint has drifted out of line, wait until it's all dry and then gently sand off any that is extraneous. Alternatively, scrape off extra paint using a razor blade.

FURNITURE FOCUS

Containers can be used to lend focus to garden furniture, which is, in itself, a feature. It could be a single piece that is a fixture of the garden, such as an old stone bench or a special garden seat; or it might be grouped seating on a patio or deck, used for relaxing or eating outside. Make a statement with a pair of urns either side of an elegant bench or use a more subtle strategy by 'accessorizing' the furniture with a planted-up container. Here, a strikingly modern garden seat, designed like a huge pod, has been set off by a low splash of colour. This is wholly appropriate, as anything more dominant would detract from, rather than complement, such a striking piece.

When cooler days put paid to long lazy days outside, outdoor furniture can be transformed into a decorative plant feature. Pretty white winter cyclamen (right) team with ornamental cabbages and windfall apples to make a delightful autumn feature of a circular metal tree seat. It's an idea you can copy with any type or style of furniture, although if you have painted wood, you'll probably need to set the pots onto co-ordinating trays, otherwise you'll soon have peeling paint. One of the advantages of using furniture is that it immediately gives your display a stage, instantly lending it more importance and bringing height variation to the whole garden.

BELOW: An unusual yet gracefully curved garden seat is perfectly complemented by the smooth lines of a stone pot planted with a glossy-leaved pittosporum and a arge stone orb.

BELOW LEFT: In late summer, the container is given an added splash of colour with Michaelmas daisies (*Aster novi-belgii*). These like to be watered well and deadheaded regularly.

ABOVE: White cyclamen (*Cyclamen coum* 'Album') and white-veined ornamental cabbages (*Brassica oleracea*) make a light and cheerful autumn combination that sets off the attractive white circular seat. Position in semi shade and keep the pots well watered.

ABOVE RIGHT: A mulch of creamy gravel topped by creamy polished river pebbles emphasizes the white theme.

CENTRE RIGHT: The pale centre of the ornamental cabbage echoes the colour theme.

BELOW AND BELOW RIGHT: When the cyclamen have finished blooming, you may want to put the corms into the garden. They can provide ground cover in the most inhospitable places, even in dry shade created by, for example, hedges or woodland areas. Left in the ground, the corms will grow up to 15cm (6in) in diameter, providing pretty autumn cover.

PARTY POTS DRESS THE GARDEN FOR A PARTY
WITH WITTY POTS THAT CAN BE PUT TOGETHER IN MOMENTS. BRING A
SENSE OF FUN TO THE OCCASION USING COLOURFUL BAGS, COFFEE CUPS
OR PRETTY PAPER. AFTER THE PARTY, PLANTS CAN FIND A PERMANENT
HOME IN A REGULAR CONTAINER OR BEDDED DOWN IN THE BORDERS.

• PARTY BAGS • SUMMER SCENTS • JUST DESSERTS • AFTER-DINNER COFFEE • SALAD DAYS

PARTY BAGS

Bag yourself a gorgeous party decoration idea for absolutely free. Gather together your favourite retail-therapy carriers and recycle them as containers for colourful summer plants. Most are fairly sturdy, so all you have to do is pop the plants in, pot and all. You could group co-ordinating bags, or, if you have a favourite store and you've collected several bags of the same design, arrange them in a line to march the length of the table, each filled with identical plants.

It's an idea that doesn't have to be confined to the table: a line of packaged plants can make a striking statement on each side of the path leading to the front door, or lined up along the patio. The real joy of this idea is it is magnificently quick and undeniably easy. The key to impact is to team the colours of the bags and plants; or to use repetition: same bags, same plants.

AFTERCARE
This is a fun but temporary idea, as water draining from the plants will soon rot the bottom of the bags. If you want to keep your party bags for any length of time, put a little saucer in the bag first. After the party, bed the plants down in the garden (or another, more permanent container). Even better, hand them to guests as goodie bags when they leave.

ABOVE: Partner your prettiest carrier bags with co-ordinating flowers to create deliciously fashionable table centres. These have been filled with a glorious combination of pink and purple blooms.

BELOW LEFT: Pretty *Pelargonium* Aristo Lavender adds a colour contrast to the aqua bag.

BELOW CENTRE: Charming *Osteospermum* 'Stardust' brings a gloriously girly feel to the arrangement.

BELOW RIGHT: Bags with extra detail, such as the addition of this ribbon, add undeniable quality.

SUMMER SCENTS

Create a seasonal sensorial delight to make your party go with a swing. Pot up fabulously aromatic lavender, redolent of long summer days, and team it with the lacy white flowers of cow parsley that so prettily dresses summer verges. Simple smooth-sided containers give an elegant, modern and fresh look to these summer-meadow favourites – ideal for gracing the patio over the summer. For entertaining, dress them up by setting them on oversized antique blue-and-white platters.

AFTERCARE

After the party, keep them watered and the lavender will reward you by blooming until late summer. The cow parsley flowers are not so long-lived, but they will self-seed around the garden for another flush of lacy flowers the following year.

RIGHT: Lavender and cow parsley teamed with antique china platters make a delightful timeless blue-and-white combination for summer parties.

BELOW LEFT: Lavender (*Lavandula* 'Imperial Gem') brings heady perfume to the table for added ambience.

BELOW CENTRE: Lacy *Orlaya grandiflora* is an elegant relative of cow parsley.

BELOW RIGHT: Deep purple flowers dancing above grey-green leaves of lavender provide timeless charm.

JUST DESSERTS

Whip up a horticultural confection for a quick-fix summer party table decoration. The easiest way to create impact is to keep it simple. Start by looking out for readily available containers that you can recycle – these little glass ramekin dishes originally contained individual chocolate puddings. Look out for other desserts that are sold in similar glass containers, such as crème brûlée, crème caramel or some organic yoghurts. They all make perfect little containers and the bonus is that they are free.

When buying plants, choose inexpensive strips of bedding plants in season so you can create impact with numbers. Once they're planted up, you can 'hide' the pots with anything from tissue or other wrapping paper, to pretty fabrics, such as translucent organza or printed cottons for a more country look. Tied up with co-ordinating ribbon, they bring charming feminine appeal to the table.

You can either group the pots for impact and use them as a central table decoration, or sit one by each place setting, then invite friends to take them home at the end of the party.

YOU WILL NEED

1 strip of summer pansies (at least 6 plants)
6 small glass ramekin dishes, or something similar
Potting compost
Green glass mulch
1 large sheet of handmade Indian paper or tissue paper
Scissors
Toning ribbon

1 Carefully plant up one pansy in each ramekin. Add a little extra compost around each pansy and press in firmly with your fingers so that it stands upright.

2 Repeat with all the other ramekins. For speed (which is always of the essence when entertaining), plant them all before going on to the next step.

3 Cover the top of the compost with a handful of green glass mulch or similar, pressing it in gently so that it does not spill over the edge of the ramekin.

ABOVE: The tones of the handmade Indian tissue paper match the pansy perfectly, adding to the colour impact of the whole arrangement.

RIGHT: Grouped together, the combination of soft tissue and pansies creates a delicate cloud of pink to decorate a summer tea table. For added height, arrange the plant parcels on a glass cake stand.

4 Place one pot at one corner of the paper, allowing enough paper all round to provide a pretty 'wrapping'. Cut out that square and use as a template to cut a further five squares of paper to the same size. Cut the ribbon into six equal lengths.

5 Place one planted-up ramekin in the centre of one square of paper and carefully gather the paper up around the sides of the container, taking care not to crush the plant.

6 Tie a ribbon around the top of the ramekin to hold the gathers in place, then smooth out any folds or creases in the paper so that it stands up. Repeat with the remaining five pots.

AFTERCARE

Pansies are fairly hardy, but with no drainage holes in the glass dishes, they may quickly become waterlogged. After the party, plant them in a garden container and they'll grow and bloom all summer.

ABOVE: Miniature pansies are an excellent choice for this project as they come in all colours of the rainbow, so there's bound to be a shade that complements your chosen tableware and linen. The soft raspberry shades of *Viola* 'Pink Gem Antique' lend a touch of nostalgia to this pretty table.

ABOVE RIGHT: The antique metal pot stand, planted with delicate variegated ivy and a few 'Pink Gem' violas, lends focus and height to the table.

RIGHT: Tone on tone, with co-ordinating tablecloth, tissue paper and petals, adds up to tablesetting success.

LEFT: Deadhead regularly and this pretty little viola will reward you with flowers all summer.

AFTER-DINNER COFFEE

Look no further than your own china cupboard
for container ideas. Coffee cups make a charming
solution because they sit well below eye level, providing
decoration without impeding conversation across the
table. These simple, zen-like square coffee cups are ideal
and beg an architectural rather than flowery treatment.
The combination of spiky grey hair grass (*Corynephorus*
'Spiky Blue') and tumbling paler sedum (*Sedum lineare*
'Variegatum'), each potted up in its own cup, makes a
smart march along the table. Alternate them, arrange
them two by two, or let the grey hair grass stand sentry
at either end of the table with the sedum taking up the
middle ranks.

AFTERCARE

The sedum can be transferred into a garden container,
or planted up on a well-drained rockery. Reaching 15cm
(6in) in height, the foliage will also trail happily from
hanging baskets and window boxes. Do not overwater.
Grey hair grass is also great in tubs, rockeries and
gravelled areas, and does not like to be overwatered.
Plant it in the ground and it will grow to 30cm (12in).

ABOVE: Make even more of a feature of this table centre by standing
the plants on a pale wooden board.

LEFT: Grey hair grass has a neat, well-groomed habit that makes a
great table decoration.

RIGHT: Lines of small pots look smart standing to attention on bench-
style refectory tables.

SALAD DAYS

Pot up something delicious in a trio of shiny long toms to add a sense of occasion to an informal barbecue in the garden and continue the food theme.

In spring and early summer, there's a wide choice of pale young salad leaves and fruits that have great visual appeal when potted up. This tasty trio of rocket leaves, cherry tomatoes and miniature strawberries is just one example. Fleshy, grass-like chives, which look especially coquettish in spring with their flirty pink pom-pom blooms, would work well, as would other herbs with attractive flowerheads. Add a little wit by using wooden picnic cutlery to label the plants.

AFTERCARE
Any produce needs space and good drainage to thrive, so after the barbecue, gently transfer the young plants into your vegetable garden or into sufficiently large containers with drainage holes. Place them in gentle sun to encourage ripening, water them well and they will reward you with delicious home-grown morsels all through the summer.

ABOVE: Young pale green rocket leaves make a neat display in the early days, but once in the garden, they'll shoot up into a tall, lanky plant, but nevertheless with delicious leaves.

LEFT: Three makes a great crowd when it comes to a display, so line them up and label them with wit.

OPPOSITE ABOVE: When putting together the display, think American diner, using clean stainless steel and fresh striped cloth.

RIGHT: The smaller varieties of strawberry have a natural charm along with the sweetest flavour.

FAR RIGHT: Green cherry tomatoes will gradually ripen if left on a sunny windowsill. Turn the fruits so that all sides can enjoy the sun.

DROUGHT BUSTERS

CLIMATE CHANGE MEANS RAIN IS NOT SUCH A REGULAR VISITOR IN MANY
REGIONS. IT'S A PARTICULAR PROBLEM FOR CONTAINERS, AS THE PLANTS
DRY OUT MORE QUICKLY THAN IN OPEN GROUND. INSTEAD OF FIGHTING
THE ELEMENTS, POT UP PLANTS WITH LESS OF A THIRST TO QUENCH.

• PRETTY PALMS • ORANGES AND LEMONS • BAMBOO TROUGH
• ORNAMENTAL GRASSES • SUCCULENTS

PRETTY PALMS

Pot up your own private desert using the beautiful palm (*Chamaerops humilis*). This striking plant can survive in temperatures as low as -10°C (14°F). However, as it is a desert plant, it's not too partial to damp, rain and fog, so unless you can find a protected spot, move it indoors for the winter months. Although the palm is at home in a dry climate, when kept in a container it doesn't develop the extreme drought resistance it would in its natural habitat. It will need regular summer watering, although it won't be as thirsty as conventional summer bedding plants. In its natural environment it can reach up to 12m (40ft) in height, but this slow grower is likely to take 15 years to reach 2m (6ft). A container of this size is fine to begin with, but as the palm grows, you will need to transfer it to a larger pot.

AFTERCARE

Place in a sunny sheltered position protected from winds. Water during the growing season, but keep fairly dry from mid autumn until early spring. In wetter areas, bring the container indoors.

YOU WILL NEED
Container
Drainage crocks
Gritty compost
Perlite
Trowel
Chamaerops humilis palm
Finely ground shell mulch
Black polished river stones

1 Gather all the 'ingredients' you need together and thoroughly water the palm. Allow the water to drain through.

2 Place a crock or two over the drainage hole in the base of the container.

3 Add compost and perlite, mixed according to manufacturer's instructions, to provide aeration and moisture retention. This will ensure good root growth and help keep the plant moist during spring and summer.

ABOVE: The smooth contours of a low terracotta urn provide contrast to the sharp leaves of the palm.

RIGHT: The spiky fronds of the palm are complemented by the tall purple *Verbena bonariensis*.

4 Using a hand trowel, mix the perlite thoroughly into the compost to ensure it is evenly distributed.

5 Carefully remove the palm from its pot, making sure you don't damage the roots. Place in the middle of the container and press compost all around the plant between the root ball and sides of the pot.

6 Using the trowel, carefully sprinkle the fine ground shell mulch on the surface of the compost.

BELOW FAR LEFT: Smooth black polished river pebbles make a shiny contrast to the fine shell mulch, bringing decoration to the base of the palm.

BELOW CENTRE LEFT: The soft purple-green tones of *Echeveria* 'Perle von Nuremburg' planted nearby complete the montage.

BELOW CENTRE RIGHT: The wonderfully firm, fanned leaves of the palm offer smart structure to the plant.

BELOW RIGHT: Container groupings can consist of more than one plant. Here a succulent provides the supporting role for the elegant starring palm.

7 Smooth the mulch with your hands to create an even, flat surface and cover all the compost.

8 Place the river pebbles around the base of the palm to create a contrasting mosaic effect.

ORANGES AND LEMONS

Citrus trees, with their fragrant flowers, glossy evergreen leaves and pretty orange or yellow fruits, make delightful container plants that can be surprisingly resilient, even withstanding the occasional light frost. However, they don't grow in a hurry, so you may well want to ring the changes over the years. Here, this 20-year-old citrus has been underplanted with lemon-scented thyme and given a mulch of Scottish cobbles for a rocky Mediterranean look. Grown in a sheltered sunny spot outdoors in London from a satsuma pip, it has taken two decades to reach 1m (3ft) in height. The hybridized fruits (which are different from the parent plant) can take over a year to mature, developing their pretty orange colour in spring.

Although citruses are traditionally brought inside during winter months in colder climes, hardened specimens can survive a mild frost, or even snowfall, though typically the fruits suffer and fall. With headily perfumed flowers appearing in the cold months and fruits ripening over the winter, these pretty trees provide interest for much of the year.

ABOVE LEFT: The decorative fruit typically ripens over the winter, though a few remain on the tree until summer.

ABOVE CENTRE: The tiny white flowers produce a strong perfume that proves irresistible to bees.

ABOVE RIGHT: Citrus trees depend on a cooler winter, and even in areas that experience a mild frost, they can thrive outside if placed in a sunny, sheltered spot.

FAR LEFT: Tiny immature green fruit will often develop at the same time as the more mature fruits are ripening.

LEFT: Lemon-scented thyme (*Thymus citriodorus* 'Aureus') makes a pretty underplanting for this little orange tree.

RIGHT: Scottish cobbles add interest to the pot and prevent soil drying out too quickly in summer.

BAMBOO TROUGH

Lend interest to the shallow riser of wide garden steps with a trough filled with houseleeks, bringing rich textural interest at ground level. Often used as a green, environmentally-friendly roof finish, even in containers houseleeks can survive on rainfall without any formal watering. This trough is made from a piece of giant bamboo, cut in half vertically. This can be sourced through wholesale plant and accessory suppliers. Although this piece does not have drainage holes, the ends are not enclosed, so excess water can run out. You may want to fix a small piece of chicken wire at each end until the plants' roots have bound in any loose compost. Make up a trough for each step, creating a feature of one of the main 'arteries' of the garden landscape.

AFTERCARE
Position in a sunny spot and do not overwater.

YOU WILL NEED
Container compost
Sharp sand
A length of large bamboo, cut in half vertically
Trowel
6 assorted houseleeks (*Sempervivum*)
4 variegated trailing ivy
2 *Euphorbia myrsinitis*
Gravel for mulch

1 Thoroughly water all the plants and allow to drain. Make up some gritty compost by mixing equal quantities of sharp sand and container compost, then almost fill the bamboo trough.

2 Carefully remove the houseleeks from their pots, and arrange them along the length of the bamboo, allowing enough space for them to thicken out.

3 In the same way, remove the trailing ivies from their pots and arrange them at intervals between the houseleeks.

4 Adjust the arrangement if necessary, making sure that the plants are evenly spaced, allowing offsets to take up space between the mother plants.

ABOVE: A tapestry of houseleeks plus some trailing ivy planted up in a trough made from a giant piece of bamboo forms a delightful planting. Set against the riser of some garden steps, it brings interest to a potentially barren site.

5 Remove the *Euphorbia myrsinitis* from their pots and arrange one at either end of the trough.

6 Carefully fill in between and around each plant with gritty compost, pressing it down carefully but firmly with your fingers.

7 Cover the surface of the compost with gravel mulch. Thoroughly water the finished planting.

ORNAMENTAL GRASSES

Ornamental grasses make excellent container subjects. Use tall stately specimens, topped with interesting seedheads, ranging from smart spikes to soft, feathery arching blooms, to create stunning focal points in the garden. As the year progresses, many grasses simply dry out, rather than die down, and can be left standing in winter, lending structure to the garden throughout the year.

Plant up a pair of matching urns or a single striking container, then stand them at a focal point, such as by the front door, on the deck or simply to mark the end of a walkway. If you want to create extra height, raise the container on a pedestal for classical impact. Many grasses are very forgiving and will thrive in poor soils with limited access to fertilizers, which is a desirable quality for any plant living within the constraints of a container.

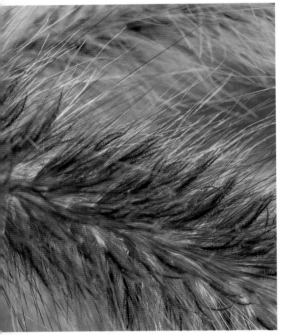

If you choose grasses that are native to drier climates, such as blue grama (*Bouteloua gracilis*), they'll need very little water. There are many grasses that don't get too thirsty, though some do need more moisture in the first year so research their needs.

As well as tall, elegant grasses, there's a wide choice of attractive shorter grasses, such as those in the miscanthus and festuca groups. Even these, with their rather more compact habit, can bring architectural interest to the garden in a different way. Wonderful blue fescues (*Festuca glauca*), or black ornamental grasses, such as *Ophiopogon planiscapus* 'Nigrescens', can look fabulous on their own in smaller containers or urns. Both are resilient and do not demand great quantities of water.

RIGHT: Stately purple fountain grass (*Pennisetum setaceum* 'Rubrum') looks breathtaking set against the copper of the urn in which it is planted. Although this is a perennial, it is often used as an annual in climates that freeze in winter. Wonderfully textural, it has a slight sheen, lending a light touch to this elegant focal point.

LEFT ABOVE AND CENTRE: The grassheads have an appealingly soft, feathery appearance, each falling into a graceful arch.

LEFT BELOW: Set on a pale brick pedestal, this container of fountain grass, which can reach 90cm (3ft) in height, takes pride of place in the garden.

SUCCULENTS

Gorgeous, glossy, architectural and very easy to please, succulents are the ideal container plants for anyone short on time. Happy to exist on very little water, they're undemanding in terms of care, but will reward you with a wonderful show of subtle colours and textures. The ultimate drought-resistant plants, most succulents hail from desert conditions where they developed various strategies to withstand the lack of water. These include leaves or stems that store water, giving them their characteristic thick leaves. However, many genuses are not frost hardy. The two most tolerant groups are houseleeks (*sempervivum*) and stonecrop (*Sedum*). Some euphorbias are also happy in colder climes.

Succulents are one of the few groups of plants that are just as happy in a container as in the ground. As they all prefer free-draining potting medium, either buy compost specially formulated for succulents, or make your own using John Innes No. 1 mixed with sharp sand (three parts compost to one part sand).

Houseleeks can be planted fairly close together, though do allow them room to thicken out over the course of a year. The individual rosettes will become larger and send out offsets which can be rooted in any spaces. These can also be used to replace any rosettes that have died away after flowering. Fertilize sparingly during the growing period. After a year, you may wish to re-pot houseleeks if they have become untidy. Stonecrop also grows well in cooler climates. Left to its own devices, it will propogate itself, filling gaps as older plants die away. However, should it become unruly, re-pot in the same way as the houseleeks.

TOP RIGHT: Succulents come in a huge array of colours, demonstrated by the soft, velvety purple of this *Echeveria* 'Perle von Nuremburg'.

CENTRE RIGHT: The combination of bright green *Sedum acre* and soft grey-green *Echeveria* 'Blue Cloud' makes an attractive drought-resistant hanging basket.

BOTTOM RIGHT: With colours like the pinks, pale greys and softest greens of this houseleek (*Sempervivum*), you can make a feature of just one plant in a pot.

FAR RIGHT: Create impact with planting by teaming pot and plant. Here, the fabulous green element of the mainly brown leaves of *Aeonium* 'Schwarzkopf' has been accentuated by pots decorated in a similar tone of green.

CROPS IN POTS THE LACK OF A
LARGE GARDEN OR LOCAL ALLOTMENT DOESN'T MEAN YOU CAN'T GROW
YOUR VERY OWN DELICIOUS, NUTRITIOUS PRODUCE. POT-GROWN SALAD
HERBS AND CONTAINER-RAISED VEGETABLES CAN EVEN FIND A PLACE ON
WINDOWSILLS AND IN FRONT GARDENS AMONGST THE FLOWERS.

• VEGETABLE BOX • CONTAINED COURGETTES • BRIGHT IDEAS
• MICRO ALLOTMENT • HERB WINDOW BOX • HERBS WITH ADDED INTEREST

VEGETABLE BOX

Looks matter when it comes to container-grown vegetables. The quantity of produce is almost certain to be restricted by space, so it's best to grow something that will look as good as it tastes. Both tomatoes and runner beans make decorative and productive candidates. Other vegetables, such as aubergines, peppers and courgettes (see page 89), may not produce large crops, but they look attractive, and it's fascinating seeing the fruits set, develop and grow over the summer.

Grow your vegetables from seed, if you have the patience and the greenhouse space, or buy young seedlings from the garden centre once they are ready to plant out towards the end of spring. Aubergines, like the plant shown here, are particularly pretty with their generous blue-green leaves and abundant ballerina-like purple flowers. You need to give them space, so choose a large trough and allow one plant for every 25cm (10in) of planting space.

YOU WILL NEED

Large trough, at least 20cm (8in) deep and 75cm (30in) wide, with drainage holes

Drainage crocks

Container compost

Water-retaining granules

3 aubergine plants

2 angelonia

1 Water the plants and allow to drain. Place crocks over the drainage holes and place plenty of compost in the bottom of the trough. Add water-retaining granules according to the manufacturer's instructions.

2 Carefully remove the aubergine from its pot and place in the trough. Repeat with the other two aubergines, positioning the plants well apart.

ABOVE: The purple aubergine flowers are most attractive, making this a delightful spring and early summer planting.

RIGHT: White angelonia has been teamed with the aubergine for purely decorative purposes. This will be especially useful as late summer approaches when all the aubergine flowers will have been removed, along with the lateral shoots, leaving a potentially denuded planting. However, by that time, the angelonia will have filled out to occupy the spaces.

3 Lift the angelonia from their pots and place in front of the aubergines. Fill in and around all the plants with compost, pressing it down firmly with your fingers.

4 Position the planted trough in a sunny spot in the garden and thoroughly water all the plants.

AFTERCARE

When the aubergines are 30cm (12in) high, pinch out the growing point to encourage a bushy habit. When five fruits have formed, remove all the side shoots and any remaining flowers. Keep moist and liquid feed on a fortnightly basis.

BELOW LEFT: Pretty as they are, aubergine blooms need to be handled with care: they have spikes on their undersides, designed to protect them from predators.

BELOW: There's something thrilling when the petals fall and there are signs that fruit has set, especially once it has grown enough to push through the sepals.

CONTAINED COURGETTES

Abundant, pretty, easy to grow and downright delicious, courgettes hit all the right buttons when it comes to growing vegetables in containers. Their generous bushy leaves quickly cover any bare earth, soon to be followed by fabulous extrovert yellow flowers and fruits, which will be ready to harvest in late summer. Courgettes are best cropped young and are delicious baked, fried, steamed or roasted.

As well as the more common long, green courgettes, seek out some of the sweeter spherical varieties, such as Tondo di Nizza, or the yellow One Ball F1, as seen here. Courgette flowers are delicious and can be fried up with the vegetable for a pretty, decorative touch. Even though the courgettes have their own flowers, these are inclined to hide under their leaves, so you can add colour and interest to the container by planting other edible flowers, such as nasturtiums, in amongst them. They'll not only pretty up the planting, but make a tasty, eye-catching addition to salads with a spicy flavour reminiscent of watercress.

Courgette seeds can be sown directly into outdoor containers from late spring, when there's no longer any chance of frost, until early summer. Alternatively, when they are readily available in garden centres, seedlings can be planted directly into the container in rich, well-fertilized compost. Keep them well watered, regularly soaking their roots.

ABOVE LEFT: These red nasturtiums (*Tropaeolum*) make a joyous combination with courgettes. However, any of the nasturtium varieties, which come in shades that range from yellow through orange to red, would work just as well.

ABOVE CENTRE: The generous yellow flowers of the One Ball F1 variety add a decorative touch both to the plant and, when cooked, to summer vegetable dishes.

ABOVE RIGHT: Planted up in an old galvanized aluminium bath, the combination of courgettes and nasturtium make a pretty, colourful pot crop.

BRIGHT IDEAS

If it's colourful potted produce you're after, you'll have plenty of choice from midsummer through to autumn. The most obvious candidate is tomatoes, which are easy to grow, thrive in containers and grow bags and, depending on the variety you choose, can produce abundant crops as long as the temperature does not drop below 12°C (55°F) at night. However, by the time the fruits start to ripen, the leaves are inclined to look a little straggly, and most are better removed if you want to expose the fruit to plenty of late summer sunshine so that it can ripen well.

Chilli peppers make delightful container plants with their red, orange and yellow fruits. In cooler climates, these need to be planted and raised under glass until the

fruits are well developed if they are to ripen into their characteristic vibrant colours.

But colour isn't confined to fruits - there are some stunning colourful leaves that thrive in pots, notably ruby chard (*Beta vulgaris*). The red-veined green leaves make a striking candidate for a potted crop as it's easy to grow, and can be harvested for salads as soon as the leaves are big enough.

ABOVE AND LEFT: The bright orange fruits of chilli peppers make a decorative container plant. In cooler climates, the season is rarely long enough to ripen them outdoors, but many garden centres offer mature chilli pepper plants, like this one which looks fabulous against the blue-green tones of an old cereal tin.

RIGHT: Ruby chard, with its vibrant stems and veins, is an astonishingly voluptuous leaf vegetable that would make an amazing display on any windowsill. It's also very easy to grow: just plant up in rich compost and keep watered, then pick off the leaves as you need them. Here, it has been tied up with toning twine to make more of a display of the stunning red stems.

MICRO ALLOTMENT

If you don't have space for a vegetable garden, make up your own mini version in a wooden box and crop the leaves for fresh home-grown salad all summer long. Arrange your produce in neat rows, just like a real market gardener. This not only makes for a more organized 'garden', but allows for easier identification and harvesting. However, as your garden grows, the divisions will be less obvious, so arrange the crops in contrasting lines.

This micro-mini market garden allows little space for much in the way of varieties, so the two main crops (lettuce and other cut-and-come-again mixed salad leaves) have been separated by the obviously different pansies (which are also edible, and make a delightful decoration for puddings and desserts). If you can obtain a larger box, you could plant several rows of pansies dividing a wider variety of container-happy crops with a small, neat growing habit, such as radish or spring onions.

AFTERCARE

Keep the plants well watered, and liquid feed every fortnight. Harvest the lettuce when it is ready, adding in another 'baby' lettuce for a repeat harvest. The salad leaves can be picked off when required.

YOU WILL NEED

Wooden box
Drainage crocks
Container compost
Water-retaining granules
Trowel
2 pansies (*Viola x wittrockiana* 'Frizzle Sizzle Yellow Blue Swirl')
1 lettuce
1 strip of mixed salad leaves

1 Thoroughly water all the plants and allow to drain. Place the crocks in the bottom of the box – here, a piece of light slate is used to cover a large crack

2 Fill the box almost to the top with compost, adding water-retaining granules following the manufacturer's instructions. Mix well, using a trowel.

3 Remove the pansies from their pots, taking care not to damage their tender roots, and position down the centre of the box.

4 Carefully position the young lettuce plant at one end of the box.

ABOVE: An old wooden salad box makes a charming container for this micro-mini market garden. The row of pansies adds colour and interest to the overall combination. Antique markets and junk shops can be a good source of similar containers. Check that the box has sufficient drainage – if the wooden slats are set tight against each other, you may need to drill a few holes in the base of the box.

5 Plant the mixed salad leaves at the other end, making sure each plant has room to grow.

6 Carefully fill in and around the plants with compost and gently press down with your fingers. Thoroughly water in.

HERB WINDOW BOX

A box of growing herbs set on the kitchen windowsill is a double delight in the summer. It not only looks pretty and smells delicious, but it's handy, too. So plant one up early in spring and enjoy the harvest right through to early autumn.

Many herbs are indigenous to Mediterranean regions, growing happily on the mountains, or even in scrubland. Majoring on scent and flavour, few are known for their colourful blooms, so when gathered together in a box, they can look a little less than decorative. However, you can make a pleasing combination by grouping herbs that have very different foliage.

Here, feathery bronze fennel stands tall next to elegant lovage and fleshy chives, whilst low-growing variegated thyme provides 'ground cover' with its pretty little leaves that will eventually fill out and trail over the side of the box. The charming alpine strawberries add colour plus delicious treats for the cook as the summer progresses.

YOU WILL NEED

Window box
Drainage crocks
Container compost
Water-retaining granules
Slow-release fertilizer
Trowel
1 chive (*Allium schoenoprasum*)

1 thyme (*Thymus citriodorus* 'Golden King')
1 bronze fennel (*Foeniculum vulgare* 'Purpureum')
1 alpine strawberry (*Fragaria vesca*)
Garden string or raffia
Fine gravel mulch

1 Water all the plants well and allow to drain. Put a layer of broken crocks and/or gravel in the bottom of the box to create good drainage. This old wooden box has large gaps between the bottom planks, so it has been first lined with newspaper.

2 Mix water-retaining granules and slow-release fertilizer into the compost, following the manufacturer's instructions. Add the compost to the window box.

3 Tip up each herb plant and carefully remove from their pots, ensuring you don't damage their roots.

4 Try positioning the plant with the largest root ball in the window box to ensure the compost level is correct. If the plant is too low in the container, then add a little more compost.

AFTERCARE

Position the box on a sunny windowsill or in partial shade. Keep moist and harvest regularly to encourage growth. Herbs retain more flavour in their leaves if any blooms are pinched out.

RIGHT: The soft blue-green aged paint on this window box is a wonderful colour for setting off foliage in all shades of green, perfectly complementing the herbs used here.

5 Arrange all the plants in the window box, then carefully fill around and between them with compost, carefully pressing it in with your fingers.

6 Bed in any strawberry offsets if there is space in the window box. If not, remove them.

7 Chives can be a bit unruly, so tie them up loosely with some lengths of garden string or raffia.

8 Finally, add some gravel mulch around the roots of the plants. This helps the compost retain moisture and makes an attractive finish to the planting.

HERBS WITH ADDED INTEREST

Fragrant and delicious, most herbs are little changed from their wild ancestors. They've never been bred by horticulturalists to produce a colourful show and, indeed, this would be counter-productive because once buds appear on a herb, it will put its energy into developing the flowers, rather than leaves loaded with flavoursome aromatic oils. So when buds do appear, it's best to pinch them out immediately, both to promote a bushy growth and to preserve the taste of the leaves.

This advice is all very practical, but it doesn't really make for the easy design of pretty baskets. However, there are many solutions. One is to combine contrasting foliage colours and textures; possibly choosing to team large-leaved purple sage with emerald-green curly parsley and low-growing golden oregano. If you do want to add colour with blooms, lavender, with its well-loved perfume and flowers, is the perfect choice. It even has a culinary right to be in a kitchen window box as it can be used to flavour sugar, biscuits and ice cream, or as a savoury substitute for rosemary.

Even in the absence of flowers, you can add decorative touches, such as plant labels, raffia-bound hearts, or simply bring interest and order by tying up unruly plants with a decorative garden twine or raffia.

LEFT: French lavender (*Lavandula stoechas*) brings colour and structure to this box of enthusiastic chives and variegated thyme. French lavender is a good choice because its flamboyant butterfly-like blooms appear earlier than the more usual garden variety, *Lavandula angustifolia*. Also, if you deadhead French lavender, it will reward you with another flush of blooms.

RIGHT: Frothy purple angelonia is not a culinary herb and therefore not edible, but it brings a decorative touch to this basket of thyme and pretty variegated sage.

PERFECT PARTNERS

CLEVER CONTAINERS DEMONSTRATE GREAT TEAMWORK. IT'S NOT
JUST ABOUT INSPIRED PLANT CHOICES; IT'S ALSO ABOUT CHOOSING
THE COLOURS, THE BALANCE BETWEEN PLANTS AND POT, AND
CREATING A LOOK THAT SUITS YOUR STYLE.

• SWEET MEADOW • NEAT TREAT • SMART CLASSIC • HANGING GARDENS
• COFFEE AND CREAM • PRETTY IN PINK • ALL ENTWINED • CHINOISERIE CHOICE
• SUMMER BLUE • ALL-SEASON INSPIRATION • FRESH START • CLASSIC URNS • LESS IS MORE

SWEET MEADOW

A favourite pot can take on quite a different personality depending on the plants you choose to put into it, looking good in gardens of very different styles. But even in the same garden you can ring the changes as the seasons turn, or take a longer view by re-inventing the planting over the years for fresh new looks.

This simple stone pot, chosen for its tall, slim lines, has been used here and in the next two projects (see pages 102–105). Its square shape lends a smart, contemporary feel, while the natural material means it could look just as at home in a cottage garden. Filled with different plant combinations not only completely changes the overall proportions, but also transforms the whole personality of the finished container.

Here, the wild charm of pretty Iceland poppies (*Papaver nudicaule*) and *Potentilla atrosanguinea* create a veritable mini-meadow. The flowers may be simple, but the strong red and yellow combination makes a confident statement that perfectly offsets the clean, modern lines of the pot.

AFTERCARE
Both plants love full sun. Keep them watered but well drained. Deadhead regularly for repeat flowering

FAR RIGHT: Tall and tangly poppies and potentilla perfectly balance the proportions of the pot, making an extrovert splash on modern decking.

TOP RIGHT AND CENTRE RIGHT: Iceland poppies bring a strong splash of impressionist colour to a cool cream deck.

BOTTOM RIGHT: Strong red potentilla flowers perfectly complement the poppies.

LEFT: Even when the petals fall, the Iceland poppies bring interest to the planting with the development of their delightful seedheads.

NEAT TREAT

Smart, low-growing houseleeks lend a neat architectural quality in complete contrast to the tall wild planting in the same pot on the previous page. It is, nevertheless, equally successful, with the delicate colours of the various varieties of houseleek (*Sempervivum*) making up an exquisite tapestry of shades, offset by a mulch of pale grey cockle shells. It's a smart, contemporary look that won't quickly overgrow, and since most houseleeks are frost resistant, they'll be happy outside in mild winters.

Over the years, the planting will become denser as each houseleek will produce offsets that will want to colonize the container. If it becomes too overcrowded, just snip off the offsets and pot up in another container (some will be needed to replace the rosettes that die back after blooming). Fill a single pot of houseleeks to use as a focal point in the garden; or plant up a pair to make a statement either side of a garden bench, the front door, or even a pathway.

YOU WILL NEED

A selection of houseleeks
(*Sempervivum*)

Container

Polystyrene plant trays or similar (see step 3)

Gravel, for drainage

Trowel

Gritty compost (made from roughly 50 per cent compost, 25 per cent sharp sand and 25 per cent gravel)

Cockle shells

1 Houseleeks are often sold as mixed varieties. They all need the same aftercare, so choose your favourites from the available selection, allowing enough to fill 90 per cent of the top of the container.

2 Thoroughly water all the plants and leave for a few hours to drain through

3 Houseleeks need good drainage and are usually planted in shallow trays. Bulk out deep pots with broken polystyrene plant trays or similar, then fill to within 15cm (6in) of the top with gravel. Top with gritty compost.

4 Arrange the houseleeks on the top of the compost, placing them fairly close together, but allowing a little room for growth.

FACING PAGE: Houseleeks occasionally put out exquisite flowers, which last for several weeks. As each one dies away, the 'parent' rosette dies with it. Carefully remove this and replace with an offset produced by one of the other houseleeks in the planting.

FAR LEFT: A combination of several varieties of houseleeks makes a glorious, easy-to-look-after planting.

TOP LEFT: The wonderful blue-green tones of some varieties have a breathtaking luminosity.

BOTTOM LEFT: Pinks and greys mingle in ripples, like waves breaking on sand.

AFTERCARE

Water sparingly. Rosettes that wither after flowering should be removed and discarded. Any offsets can be removed from the parent plant once roots have developed and replanted in a space in the container or elsewhere.

5 Using a small trowel, carefully fill between and around each plant with gritty compost, making sure each one is well bedded in.

6 Press the compost down firmly with your fingers, adding more where needed.

7 Finally, add a mulch of pretty cockle shells as here (available from craft shops or fishmongers), or, alternatively, gravel.

SMART CLASSIC

Inspired by classical Italian gardens, topiary can make a city-smart statement at a front door, on a verandah, or as a focal point in a larger garden setting. This bay orb, underplanted with neat, colourful hebes, creates yet another, completely different look for the container featured on pages 100–103.

The tailored look of topiary is perfectly complemented by the simple geometric lines of the container. Evergreen hebe brings interest to the lower third of the trunk which would otherwise be bare, producing pretty purple blooms during late summer and early autumn, while the addition of trailing variegated ivy softens the top edge for a composition that will look good throughout the year. The tall, tailored profile of the overall combination is elegant enough on its own. Smarter still, plant up a pair of containers for the front door, or several to arrange in lines along a pathway.

YOU WILL NEED

Container
Drainage crocks or gravel
Potting compost
Slow-release fertilizer
1 standard bay tree (*Laurus nobilis*)

4 *Hebe* 'Autumn Glory' or dwarf hebe
4 variegated trailing ivy
Polished pink pebble mulch

1 Water the plants well. Put a layer of crocks or gravel at the bottom of the pot for good drainage. Part-fill the container with compost, add fertiliser granules in quantities according to manufacturer's instructions and mix with compost. Position the tree in the pot.

2 Carefully remove each hebe from its container. If it is very tightly packed in, squeeze the container first to help ease it out.

3 Carefully arrange one hebe at each corner of the container, around the tree trunk.

4 Add a trailing ivy plant to each corner. In-fill between and around each plant with compost. Press in firmly with your fingers.

ABOVE AND ABOVE RIGHT: 'Autumn Glory' is one of the easiest hebe varieties to grow in almost any soil and produces pretty purple flowers from summer through to late autumn.

RIGHT: Clipped bay is a classic choice for the front door. Underplant with purple hebes for a colourful twist that will look equally good in a smart city or casual country location.

5 Finish the pot with a mulch of polished pebbles – these pink ones perfectly complement the hebe blooms. Water well.

AFTERCARE

Keep in a sunny position or partial shade. Water when the surface compost is dry to the touch. Do not allow to dry out. The container will restrict the hebes' growth, keeping them compact, but cut back any leggy growth after flowering. After a couple of years, you might want to plant them in the garden where they will grow to nearly 80cm (3ft).

HANGING GARDENS

If you thought hanging baskets were the mainstay of cottage gardens, think again. Even given the same basket, you can create quite different looks, depending on the plants you choose. This cornucopia basket is an excellent choice for design flexibility. Its conical shape brings an architectural quality to the whole planting, suiting both pretty combinations of summer blooms and more modern teams of succulents or grasses.

Whatever style you choose, aim for a pleasing proportion between plants and basket – two-thirds container to one-third planting is an elegant choice. If you pick plants that grow upwards, aim for a height that is two-thirds the length of the container; alternatively, baskets featuring low-growing trailing plants that spill over the sides look pleasing if the overall effect is one-third planting to two-thirds container.

ABOVE LEFT: Tumbling succulents *Sedum acre* and *Echeveria* 'Blue Cloud' and sedum create a smart, modern evergreen solution. Plant them up using compost mixed with a third sharp sand to create good drainage. Do not allow the basket to dry out.

ABOVE: A delightful single begonia in vermillion red makes a joyous basket, tumbling over the sides of the cornucopia and bringing a splash of colour to a dark corner.

RIGHT: Shades of lavender and lilac make a pretty late summer combination. *Aster novi-belgii* offers the stronger purple focus, set against a froth of paler lilac angelonia. Keep them well watered for late summer colour.

COFFEE AND CREAM

Summer pots don't have to toe the traditional bedding line. Here the combination of a tall modern stone pot, leggy ligularia and a confection of heucheras in punchy lime and soft caramel with spears of ornamental maize (*Zeamays*), makes a dramatic statement. Fit for gardens both conventional and modern, it's strong enough to occupy a focal point, but protect from slugs if you want to keep the ligularia looking perfect.

AFTERCARE

Place in a sunny position and keep well watered. Protect from slugs. Cut down ligularia to the ground in autumn, but leave the heuchera to provide colour throughout the winter months.

YOU WILL NEED

Container
Drainage crocks
Potting compost
Water-retaining granules
Slow-release fertilizer

1 *Ligularia dentata*
1 maize (*Zeamays*)
3 *Heuchera* 'Key Lime Pie'
3 *Heuchera* 'Crème Brûlée'

1 Water the plants and allow to drain. Cover the drainage hole with a crock. Fill the lower third of the pot with compost. Add water-retaining granules and fertilizer according to instructions and mix well. Place the ligularia in the centre of the pot.

2 Add the maize, positioning it carefully to complement the ligularia.

3 Position the heucheras, alternating the 'Key Lime Pie' with the softer tones of 'Crème Brûlée'.

4 Fill the space between the plants with compost and press in lightly with your fingers. Once satisfied with the planting, water the pot generously.

TOP LEFT: Set out all the components of the planting to help you visualize the colour and form of the combination.

TOP: The caramel undersides of the dramatic ligularia leaves, complement the tones of *Heuchera* 'Crème Brûlée'.

ABOVE: This bronze-toned maize works well with the ligularia, providing complementary interest to the planting.

RIGHT: A 'carpet' of heucheras, in lime green and caramel tones, sets off the dramatic leaves of the tall ligularia.

PRETTY IN PINK

Pot up a miniature cottage garden for all-summer colour on windowsills, patios, decks or garden tables. All the combinations shown here are based around classic summer container plants which have become favourites for a very good reason – they work! Traditional bedding such as petunias, pansies, verbena and lobelia have earned their top position because, when planted up in spring and watered well, they reward us with continuous blooms right through to the end of summer. Garden pests are disinterested in them and they're generally resistant to disease.

Highly versatile, these popular plants are available in a wide variety of colours from soft, subtle dusky shades to vibrant brights, offering plenty of scope for endless combinations. The more delicate, muted tones exude cottage charm when planted up in timeless terracotta such as this basketweave pot, whilst the more zingy hues planted in shiny stainless steel or zinc suit a more modern setting.

YOU WILL NEED
Container
1 patio rose (*Rosa* 'Sweet Cover')
1 *Calibrachoa* Million Bells Cherry Blossom
3 pansies (*Viola* 'Amber Kiss')
3 *Helichrysum* 'Yellow'
Potting compost
Slow-release fertiliser
Water-retaining granules
Gravel, for drainage

AFTERCARE
Position in full sun. Water and deadhead regularly.

1 Water all the plants. Put some gravel in the pot for good drainage. Mix fertilizer and water-retaining granules into compost, according to the manufacturer's instructions. Part-fill the pot.

2 Place the rose to the back of the pot, then add the Million Bells in front of it.

3 Add the helichrysum to fill out the planting and provide a trailing element.

4 Add the pansies to the container. Fill in and around the plants with extra compost and press in well with your fingers. Water well.

ABOVE LEFT: Gather all your 'ingredients' together. Water the plants well and allow them to drain before planting up your container.

ABOVE: Based around a patio rose, this cottagey planting looks enchanting combined with Million Bells, helichrysums and pansies in soft antique tones.

TOP RIGHT: Two containers using exactly the same plants in different colourways give different end results. At the top, surfinia petunias and verbenas in soft coral tones plus limey lysimachia are perfectly complemented by a soft terracotta pot.

ABOVE RIGHT: The same plants but this time the vibrant tones are set off by stainless steel.

ALL ENTWINED

Combine a pair of climbers in a pot for delightful all-summer colour on the deck or patio, or to add colour where it's lacking in the border. This is a perfect example: the beautiful blue *Clematis* 'Cézanne' flowers from late spring to early autumn, to be joined in midsummer by the solanum which produces a continuous flush of frothy white blooms until early autumn. And when they're over, the semi-evergreen leaves of the solanum keep the colour going right through milder winters. The simple modern container perfectly offsets the enthusiastic floral energy it contains, while its soft blue tones strengthen the colour impact of the clematis' blooms. Left to their own devices, the plants will become completely entwined and impossible to separate without cutting the plants down to the ground. So plant them up in a generously-sized container, allowing them plenty of room to expand.

AFTERCARE

Place the container in full sun. Water well in dry spells. Regularly deadhead the clematis flowers.

YOU WILL NEED

1 *Clematis* 'Cézanne'	Container compost
1 *Solanum laxum* 'Album'	Slow-release fertilizer
Container	Water-retaining granules
Metal obelisk	Garden string
Drainage crocks	

ABOVE: Enhance the colour impact of the overall combination with a container that echoes the hues of the plants.

RIGHT: As they grow, the clematis and solanum stems will twist around one another, filling the metal frame with their flowers.

1 Thoroughly water both the plants and leave for a couple of hours before planting up to allow them to drain. Push the metal frame into the pot, making sure it is held securely. If you choose a larger pot, you'll need to put the compost in before positioning the frame.

2 Place a crock over the drainage hole, then mix some fertilizer and water-retaining granules, following the manufacturer's instructions, with enough compost to fill the pot. Place a layer in the bottom of the pot, then position the solanum in the pot inside the frame.

3 Add the clematis to the pot inside the frame. Fill in and around plants with compost, pressing it down firmly with your fingers.

4 Tie in the plants using soft green garden string. Do not use garden wire ties as these could damage the tender stems.

CHINOISERIE CHOICE

Exotic inspiration from the Far East provides an exciting way to inject vibrant colour into the garden. Prompted by a traditional Chinese colour scheme, this shiny black lacquer-like pot has been filled with the fabulous clashing pink and hot red tones of readily-available and easy-to-grow fuchsias and dahlias. Set against a turquoise background, such as painted garden furniture, the authentic Chinese colour combination is complete.

This is a statement combination, so don't be shy. Think big: invest in the largest pot you can, and plan to use several dahlias and at least two fuchsias. Given plenty of fertilizer, they'll reward you with flamboyant flowers from midsummer until early autumn, spanning that slightly barren period when the summer blooms are over and autumn is yet to produce its abundant colour.

Very large pots, like this one, are extremely heavy even when empty. To lighten the load and provide extra drainage, add some cut-up plant trays to the bottom of the pot.

AFTERCARE

Position in full sun and use liquid fertilizer weekly. Pinch out the tips of the dahlias to encourage a bushy habit. Keep watered and deadhead any blooms for repeat flowering throughout the season. When the first frost blackens the dahlia leaves, lift the tubers, dry them and dust them down with fungicide, then store in a dry, well-ventilated place. Alternatively, move the whole container under glass.

YOU WILL NEED

Large, glossy black pot
Drainage crocks
Old plant trays, or similar (see step 1)
Scissors
Container compost
Slow-release fertilizer
Moisture-retaining granules
Trowel
2 *Dahlia* 'Karma Lagoon'
2 *Dahlia* 'Dark Angel'
2 *Fuchsia* 'Mrs Popple'

1 Thoroughly water the plants and allow to drain. Place a crock over the drainage hole. Add some cut-up plastic plant trays to the bottom of the pot.

2 Almost fill the pot with compost, add fertilizer and moisture-retaining granules, according to the manufacturer's instructions, and mix in well with a trowel.

3 Arrange the larger 'Karma Lagoon' dahlias in the pot, making a pleasing arrangement.

4 Add the 'Dark Angels' dahlias, deadheading any blooms that are already past their best.

ABOVE: Extrovert containers like this one are strong enough to hold their own, even within a garden setting that features quite different tones. Think of it as an outdoor flower arrangement, bringing a concentration of colour just where it is needed.

ABOVE RIGHT: The vibrant magenta shades of the dahlias continue the Chinese theme of this planting.

5 Then position the fuchsias to fill the space left between the dahlias.

6 Infill compost between the plants using the hand trowel and press in with your fingers. Water well.

SUMMER BLUE

Blue and white make a glorious combination and in summer there is a wide choice of bedding in all shades of blue, ranging from pastel baby blue to deepest indigo. You can either choose to concentrate on a single tone, such as this rich purply-blue, or mix several different shades. If mixing, try to combine three or more shades as two slightly mismatched blues can look like a mistake. The addition of a little white brings the blues to life, appearing to intensify the colour.

This choice of petunias, verbenas and lobelia guarantees vibrant, easy-to-care-for colour from late spring right through to early autumn. All these varieties simply continue growing, creating a tumbling combination of an ever-increasing number of blooms as the season progresses. In practical terms, to keep the pot looking at its best, this means deadheading is a daily task by midsummer.

AFTERCARE
Water regularly: during the sunny months, this is likely to be every day. Deadhead daily for repeat blooming.

ABOVE: A simple basket trough makes an excellent cottage-style container for this pretty country combination. Its grey tones lend a soft driftwood effect, perfectly complementing the bright blues.

TOP LEFT: Purple verbena brings structure to the planting, plus the intense colour of their compact flowers.

CENTRE LEFT: Surfinia petunias are summer basket mainstays, and with good reason: they offer an endless succession of blooms, becoming ever more trailing as the season progresses.

BOTTOM LEFT: Mixed trailing lobelia offers a fascinating combination of blue and white flowers all on the same plant.

RIGHT: Blousy petunias provide a wonderful textural contrast to the pristine clusters of tiny verbena blooms.

ALL-SEASON INSPIRATION

The key to planning container arrangements that will last all year is to dovetail plants which provide interest in the summer with those that come into their own during the colder months. Here, smart evergreen *Skimmia japonica* 'Rubella' provides elegant structure all year, perfectly offsetting the exquisite pure white beauty of *Begonia* 'Double White' and its little cousin *Begonia* 'Ambassador', which bloom flamboyantly all summer. By the end of the summer, the skimmia is producing its buds, ready to bloom when the begonias decide it's time to rest.

Although the skimmia blooms right through the winter, adding some bulbs between and around the plants when potting up would bring welcome extra interest in the spring. This would create most impact if you co-ordinate the blooms with the rest of the planting: try pretty white daffodils, such as 'Ice Follies' or 'Thalia', followed by tulips 'Spring Green', which are white with green stripes.

AFTERCARE

Position in shade or semi-shade. Keep the plants well watered in the summer, but water more sparingly during the winter months.

ABOVE: Both the skimmia and begonias have smart, shiny leaves that give the planting structure.

RIGHT AND FAR RIGHT: The pure white *Begonia* 'Double White' and single *Begonia* 'Ambassador' blooms add a glamorous feminine touch.

FRESH START

Not all containers are one-season wonders. You may well have kept a favourite plant in a container for years, and want to 'update' it a little. Even if there's only a little spare space in the pot, this is not difficult to do, especially if you seek out the smaller bedding plants, such as violas.

This agapanthus is a perfect example of this planting trick. It typically takes a couple of years to flower, so although its forest of lush leaves is attractive enough, a little splash of colour is always welcome. During its first summers, pretty little blue violas were planted amongst the leaves. It was a habit that continued, and each year, even once the agapanthus started booming, it was underplanted with a selection of violas. At the end of the season, they were removed, allowing space for next year's fresh intake.

AFTERCARE

Position in full sun. Keep moist but well drained. Deadhead the violas regularly. Agapanthus flowers transform into spectacular globe-like seedheads, bringing autumn interest.

YOU WILL NEED
Potted *Agapanthus* 'Lilliput'
Slow-release fertilizer
Small quantity of potting compost
Trowel
4 *Viola* 'Columbine'
2 *Helichrysum* 'Yellow'

1 Water all the plants and allow to drain. Mix some fertiliser into the compost, following the manufacturer's instructions. Remove any weeds from the potted agapanthus.

2 Using a small trowel, make a hole in the compost large enough to plant one viola.

3 Repeat with other violas and the helichrysum. Top dress the pot with the fertilized compost.

LEFT: *Agapanthus* 'Lilliput' is
a small, but equally vibrant
version of the giant *Agapanthus
africanus*.

RIGHT: Agapanthus prefers not
to be transplanted into a bigger
pot. The tighter its root ball,
the more blooms it produces.
So leave it in its pot and add
interest each summer. Here,
tiny blue violas echo the blue of
the agapanthus blooms, whilst
the helichrysum adds a vibrant
lime-green touch.

BELOW: Pretty flecked *Viola*
'Columbine' tone well with the
agapanthus, bringing extra
colour down amongst the
lower leaves.

CLASSIC URNS

Introduce an urn or two into your garden for elegant decoration that dates back to Ancient Greece and beyond. Classic Italian landscaping often included huge urns, positioned in focal points, or in lines on pedestals to create vistas through grand European gardens, both in ancient Roman times and in the neoclassical period of the eighteenth century. Even if your garden dimensions don't quite measure up to that scale, you can be sure an urn or two will lend a timeless, elegant touch to your outdoor space.

Use a single large urn as a focal point, such as at the end of a path, or to mark the central point of a knot. Pairs can be used to mark a path, patio area or gateway, whilst smaller urns can be used as garden table decorations. Choose stone, metal or even lead and fill them with flowering plants for a seasonal summery look, or foliage for a more architectural theme.

ABOVE: The styling and mossy look of this green urn is reminiscent of Ancient Greece so it has been planted with a cardoon – a motif that is often seen in classical architecture.

LEFT: Black grasses *Ophiopogon planiscapus* 'Nigrescens' planted into a pair of white-painted metal urns make a strong, modern statement.

RIGHT: Groups often create greater impact. Here, three urns with a rusty appearance are complemented by aged metal crown to create an enchanting montage set against a lush jungly spot. Two have been planted with oxalis, and one black grass.

LESS IS MORE

A mass of blooms all from the same plant can create great impact, so if a clever combination does not seem appropriate in a particular situation, don't be afraid of using single-variety plantings in large quantities. The key to success lies in choosing a container that complements both the colour and the habit of the plants.

A favourite container in a colourful hue is always a good starting point, then simply scour your local garden centre for seasonal bedding plants to tone. Another quick and easy way to make a colour link

between pot and plant is to paint up a container to match the blooms (see page 12 for instructions). Make it plain or patterned: it needn't be difficult if you employ the help of stencils or stamps, or simply go for geometrics using masking tape to help create the pattern.

ABOVE: Vibrant *Verbena* 'Homestead Purple' is perfectly complemented by an elegant, modern geometrical container in a lively blue. Positioned in full sun or partial shade and regularly watered, it will reward you with abundant flowers from early summer through to autumn.

LEFT: Single begonias are sweet, simple flowers and, en masse, they can be utterly charming, so gather together a multitude in an old galvanized bathtub. The utilitarian character of the bath combined with a froth of flowers spilling out of the top has a cottage charm that stops well short of fussy.

RIGHT: The greenish tinge of these white petunias lends a touch of the exotic to a can't-go-wrong variety. Packed into a simple stone container, they will produce a glorious show of flowers from late spring until early autumn.

When planting, don't hold back from packing in a generous quantity of annual bedding plants. You'll be amply rewarded with a lush finished result and if you've mixed plenty of slow-release fertilizers and water-retaining granules in with the compost, there'll be enough goodness in the container to support the plants until the end of the season (just remember to deadhead frequently). Evergreens and perennials, however, which may be resident in the same container for one, two or even three years, will thank you for a bit more space.

RIGHT: A shiny, deep purple pot perfectly complements bright pink *Cosmos* 'Sensation' for colour all summer. Positioned in front of bright yellow border flowers intensifies the pink of the cosmos and sets off its yellow centres.

BELOW RIGHT: *Fuchsia* 'Thalia', with its slender flowers and generous leaves, is quite different from its more flamboyant cousins that we recognize so well. Usually grown as a specimen plant, this one has been potted up in a Grecian-style urn, lending it the sense of importance it so richly deserves.

BELOW LEFT: A lead container makes the ideal partner for fabulous silvery-leaved ferns. Position in shade or partial shade and keep well watered for the best results.

INDEX

ACKNOWLEDGEMENTS

Tessa and Debbie would like to thank Fenella Fudge and Sarah McDermott for kindly allowing us to photograph their lovely gardens and Dan Curran for letting us photograph at Ginkgo Gardens.

Thanks, too, to Dan Curran, Paul Tucker and Shane Kennealy for all their help with identifying plants.

Thanks to Paul Tucker at Ginkgo Gardens for his inspired plantings: Hanging Gardens on page 106; Summer Blue, page 116, All-Season Inspiration on page 117.

Ginkgo Gardens

Landscape design and garden centre

Ravenscourt Park

London W6 0SL

020 8563 7112

www.ginkgogardens.co.uk